Praise for
The Art of Selling to the Affluent

"Shockingly professionals are still following the advice of the sales gurus of yesteryear who preached the importance of 'asking for referrals' Yet, when is the last time anyone responded to this question by immediately jotting down the name, number, and e-mail address of a good friend or family member? Matt Oechsli has tapped into the mindset of the affluent, helping marketers and sales professionals understand the far more subtle techniques that build long-term loyal clients who happily refer—without being asked. *The Art of Selling to the Affluent, Second Edition* is an easy read with actionable takeaways. It cements the fact that relationship management strategies, combining business and social interactions, are the secret to an endless source of introductions."

> —Susan Theder, Chief Marketing Officer, Cetera Financial Group

"As a former sales trainer of a *Fortune 500* company and currently the president of a company that consults with firms who are attempting to sell their services to the government, it is rare that I read a book on sales that tells me anything I don't already know. *The Art of Selling to the Affluent, Second Edition* is a definite exception of the rule. Matt Oechsli not only understands sales at a granular level, he's done his homework on the affluent consumer. This book will become a core part of every sales training curriculum that is targeting the affluent."

> —David Claiborne, President, Winning Proposals

"Love, love, love this book! Thank you Matt, you did it again. Relevant, insightful, practical ways to fine tune our practice to best serve today's affluent client."

> —Jo-Ann Sloan, Managing Broker, Premier Sotheby's International
> Realty and National Real Estate Sales Trainer

"Wow, did I just learn a serious lesson: the importance of getting personal with affluent clients and prospects—even in the IT world. We produce and sell a product that is both highly technical and sophisticated in a very competitive field—and we landed one of our largest clients by following the principles Matt has outlined in this book. *The Art of Selling to the Affluent, Second Edition* is required reading for my entire sales team."

> —Dan Vena, National Sales Manager, Claysys Technical Solutions

"Matt Oechsli does it again! With the Great Recession creating a new normal, nothing is more important than staying current with how people with wealth make major purchasing decisions. The fact that everything contained in these chapters is based on current research sets this book apart. Like Oechsli's previous book, this is a must read for anyone attempting to sell anything to today's affluent consumer."
—Rich Santos, Group Publisher, Wealthmanagement.com, the digital resource for REP. and Trusts and Estates

"Matt Oechsli delivers strategic and tactical tools throughout this book that will enable those who compete in the affluent/high net-worth space to participate with an edge."
—Tim McKinney, VP ADT Security Services, Custom Home

The ART *of* SELLING *to the* AFFLUENT

HOW TO ATTRACT, SERVICE, AND RETAIN WEALTHY CUSTOMERS AND CLIENTS FOR LIFE

second edition

MATT OECHSLI

WILEY

Contents

Chapter 1 The World of Today's Affluent 1

Profile of Today's Affluent 5

Affluent Macro Shifts 7

About This Book 8

The Research behind This Book: 2012 and 2013

   Affluent Purchasing Decision Research 12

Summary 13

Chapter 2 The Affluent Mind-Set Shift 15

Pre- and Postcrisis Decision Making 21

Pre- and Postcrisis Lifestyles 23

Summary 24

Chapter 3 Wowing Today's Affluent 27

Your "Wow" Service Experience 30

Surprise and Delight: A Simple Way to Wow

   Affluent Clients 31

The Law of Reciprocity   32
Uncovering Client Information   34
Summary   39

Chapter 4   Affluent Buzz Factor   41
Hosting an Intimate Client Event   45
Reasons to Avoid Large-Scale Client Events   46
Three Objectives   48
Five Steps to Activate Affluent Buzz via
    Intimate Events   50
Intimate Event Planning Form   55
Social Media   58
Visibility Campaign   61
Getting Involved   62
Social Prospecting   64
Revisiting Past Opportunities   66
Beware! Top Five Ways Salespeople
    Appear Salesy   67
Summary   70

Chapter 5   Building Personal Relationships   73
Referrals versus Introductions   77
Professional Alliances   81
Getting Personal   83
Becoming Social   85
Cultivate Personal Relationships   87
The Digital Impact   88
Keep It Simple and Personal   91
Summary   93

Chapter 6   Creating the Right First Impression   95
The Great Recession's Impact   97
The Impact of Environment   99
The Power of Personal Presence   100
Exuding Gravitas (Power Pose)   101
How to Make a Good First Impression   103
A Handful of Simple Tips   105
Summary   112

Chapter 7   Today's Affluent Female   115
Teachable Moments   118
Paradise Lost   121

The Affluent Female's "Gift of Gab"   124
Top Turnoffs   125
Five Steps to Strengthen Your Relationships with
   Affluent Women   126
Female to Female   127
Connecting   128
Summary   129

Chapter 8   The Emerging Affluent   131
The Generational Divide   133
Word-of-Mouth Power through Social Media   135
Decision Making   136
Communication   139
Generational Similarities   141
Summary   142

Chapter 9   The Amazon Effect   145
The Apple Experience   150
Online Research   151
Summary   158

Chapter 10   How to Move Upmarket   161
America on $250,000 a Year   166
The Working Affluent   168
Mind-Set   169
Knowledge   170
Opportunity   171
P.S.: Create Opportunities   171
Worst Fear Exercise   172
Summary   174

Chapter 11   Overcoming Affluent Sales Reluctance   175
Thou Shalt Overcome   178
Is This a Problem?   179
Taking Action   180
Controlling the Devilish Voice of Doubt   183
Summary   190

Chapter 12   Maximizing Your Affluent
   Sales Opportunities   193
Can You Envision Your Affluent Future?   197
Closing the Gaps   199
Activating Your Achievement Cycle   201

Achievements of the Past   202
Staying on Your Critical Path   206
Four Key Traits of Top Affluent
   Sales Professionals   212
Summary   216

*Appendix: The 12 Commandments of
       Affluent Selling   219*
Index   235

Chapter 1 The World of Today's Affluent

Sometimes, what the affluent *don't* do speaks volumes.

For almost a year, Mr. and Ms. "Elliot" observed the construction of a beach house across the street from their vacation home. On the way to the shore, they often stopped to talk with the owner, "Brad," as he supervised the building contractors.

Brad was always up for a neighborly chat. He loved talking about the quality of the building materials and the workmanship. He loved giving tours of the house as it rose from the vacant lot. This was his family's third house—his retirement home on the beach.

One day, however, Brad stopped coming to the house. Instead, a Realtor's sign appeared in the front yard. The sign stayed there for many months until it, like Brad, simply vanished.

At this point, Ms. Elliott asked Mr. Elliot for his views on purchasing the property. After all, they knew the house was high quality. They'd inspected every square inch of the place. What's more, while their current beach home would be great for their children, it wasn't something she wanted for their retirement years. Why not purchase the luxury beach house, and let the kids stay in the old house during their visits?

Two hours (and a few phone calls) later, Mr. Elliot negotiated a cash deal for the beach house, which included all of the furnishings. Two weeks later, they closed on the house.

What the Elliots *did* was straightforward. They bought a house. What the Elliots *didn't* do is less obvious, but it illustrates: (1) how today's affluent make major purchase decisions, (2) who makes the decisions, and (3) whom they trust. Note the following:

- The Elliots did not seek counsel from their financial advisor before buying the house. Scarred by the recent financial crisis and the "Great Recession," they no longer had full faith and confidence in their advisor's ability to manage all their assets.

- They did not contact the Realtor (the one who planted the sign) to broker the deal. Instead, they went directly to the owner—someone they knew, liked, and trusted.
- Mr. Elliot (the traditional "pater familias") did not initiate the deal. Ms. Elliot spearheaded the purchase and had the final say.
- As of this writing, the Elliots have not informed their siblings and friends of the purchase. Ms. Elliot's explanation was simple: "I don't want anyone getting the wrong impression [the impression that we're wealthy]."

Is every affluent household like Mr. and Ms. Elliot's?

No, but the Elliots *are* representative of how affluent consumers make major investment and purchase decisions in today's climate—in the new world produced by the Great Recession.

Since 2008, the economic landscape has radically changed, and nobody is more aware of this than the nation's affluent households. Bernie Madoff and his Ponzi scheme; financial products so complex that few people understood the risks; a government that failed to oversee and regulate financial institutions; people taking out mortgages they couldn't afford . . . nobody paid closer attention to these calamities (and their aftermath) than the affluent.

As a result, affluent attitudes have undergone a metamorphosis. Among other things, the affluent are much more discriminating and much more skeptical than they once were, and this skepticism requires companies to dramatically adjust their marketing and sales practices. Keep in mind the following. . . .

Today's affluent don't trust salespeople (they'll say anything).

They don't trust politicians (of either party). They're skeptical of large corporations (too big to fail). They don't trust the news media (entertainers exploiting people's fears).

Despite this cynicism and the drubbing they received during the financial crisis, the affluent are back—with plenty of cash to spend. They're making major purchases with greater frequency than any other population segment. While some nonaffluent consumers have retreated from the stores, the stock market, and real estate markets, the affluent are marching forward. While many people learned nothing from the financial and real estate debacles, the affluent have adjusted their attitudes and behaviors to ensure they won't make the same mistakes again. While prosperous households have money to spend and the will to spend it, the average salesperson had better learn how to earn this group's confidence if he or she hopes to benefit.

Without a doubt, the ability to close deals with well-heeled consumers is an invaluable skillset for any entrepreneur or salesperson. Selling to the affluent is a great way to become affluent yourself. But that's easier said than done.

The Realtor who listed that luxury beach house should have cleaned up, but she blew it—big time. She blew it because she approached the job in a perfunctory, "paint-by-numbers" manner—like a zombie imitating the motions of a living salesperson. She listed the home, staged open houses, and showed the property to interested parties.

Yawn. A robot could have done that.

With just a little extra effort, this Realtor *could* have cultivated relationships with homeowners in the area, asking if they knew of anyone who might want to join the neighborhood. She *could* have initiated a word-of-mouth buzz, spreading the news to dozens of prospective buyers that a handsome piece of real estate was suddenly available—a property unlikely to *stay* available for very long.

Had the Realtor done this, she might have connected with Ms. Elliot. She might have accelerated interest in the house, brokered the sale, and earned a hefty commission. Instead, this Realtor—like many salespeople—didn't have the slightest idea what makes the affluent tick. In fact, she didn't even *know* that she didn't know.

PROFILE OF TODAY'S AFFLUENT

So who are the "the affluent" and what makes them tick?

For one, they are highly educated. Fifty-five percent have a graduate degree. Thanks to this level of education (and the lessons they learned from the financial crisis), the affluent are the savviest of all American consumers.

For the purposes of our research, we define affluence based on two criteria; participants must meet one or both to be considered affluent:

1. *Investable assets ($500,000 or greater).* We find it helpful to start with $500,000 in investable assets as the baseline. Many salespeople targeting the affluent are looking for "million-aires," a group that took a nosedive with the collapse of the stock market in late 2008 to a low of 2.26 million individuals with $1 million or greater in investable assets in the United States. Yet, as the economy recovered, so did the number of millionaires; up to 3.44 million in 2012.[1] Note: Investable assets are not synonymous with *net worth*. The assets must be so liquid that the family can apply the funds toward a major purchase or investment with relative ease and speed.

2. *Household income ($250,000 or greater).* The higher the household income, the greater the purchasing power. Today's affluent households are purchasing more goods and services than their nonaffluent counterparts, which is why salespeople should master the art of selling to this key demographic.

Adjusted to 2011 dollars, the Congressional Budget Office (CBO) calculated that in 1990 the minimum required for being one of America's top-quintile income earners was $92,092. In 2011 the entry point had risen to $101,582. In other words, the top-quintile household has at least $9,490 more to spend today than it did 21 years ago.

If we focus on just the top 5 percent of income earners, we learn that households had at least $27,943 more to spend in 2011 than in 1990: $186,000 versus $158,057.

The affluent are spending more money today because they have more money to spend.

---

[1]2012 CapGemini World Wealth Report.

AFFLUENT MACRO SHIFTS

Two key findings reveal how the Great Recession fundamentally changed the affluent approach to major purchases. Not surprisingly, both findings hinge on trust:

1. *The gender shift:* Ms. Elliot isn't the only woman spearheading major financial decisions in affluent households. For various reasons, affluent females are taking a more active role in every aspect of their families' finances.

   According to our research, affluent women assign greater importance than their male counterparts to metrics, including communication, personalized service, and trust. If the woman of an affluent household wants a new kitchen, her husband might be tapped to negotiate with the contractors, but the woman will probably call the shots. If she has reservations or complaints about the contractor, she'll dump the company in a heartbeat, regardless of her husband's opinion.

   Whether an investment involves real estate, landscaping, remodeling, automotive purchases, jewelry, travel, or a cruise, the salesperson must understand the needs, wants, and expectations of the female heads of affluent households.

2. *The relationship shift:* The second affluent macro shift involves client relationships. For example, our research on *trustworthiness in advertising* rankings of financial advisors show that only 44 percent earn "some to full trust" from affluent clients. This places them on the same level as automotive salesmen (at 42 percent).

I know many outstanding financial advisors, but since the profession as a whole received an unfavorable survey ranking, it illustrates the magnitude of the affluent attitude shift, especially when we divide advisor–client relationships into two categories: (1) purely business, and (2) business and personal.

   We uncovered a strong correlation between positive client attitudes and having a business-and-personal relationship with the salesperson. If an affluent client feels she has also developed a personal relationship with, for example, her financial advisor, her overall assessment of the advisor tends to skyrocket. Consider the following from our survey regarding financial advisors. The percentages shown reflect those who rate their advisor as performing "very well" to "extremely well":

- Being trustworthy, having our family's best interests at heart

Rankings:		
	Business relationship only	38%
	Business and personal relationship	61%

- Delivering high-level personal service

Rankings:		
	Business relationship only	41%
	Business and personal relationship	63%

- Providing timely, not mechanical communication

Rankings:		
	Business relationship only	42%
	Business and personal relationship	61%

- Meeting investment performance expectations

Rankings:		
	Business relationship only	30%
	Business and personal relationship	45%

Client confidence increases dramatically when the advisor cultivates a business-and-personal relationship with the client. This statistical phenomenon applies to many different industries and professions.

Whether you sell real estate, jewelry, or luxury cruises—regardless of whether most of your client encounters are face-to-face or digital—developing personal relationships with your affluent clients is *key* to success. At the very least, the salesperson that expands his or her relationship beyond "strictly business" is more likely to stimulate positive word-of-mouth recommendations from clients—and personal referrals are the salesperson's best friend.

ABOUT THIS BOOK

This book introduces you to the new affluent consumers, acquainting you (or reacquainting you) with strategies and tactics that will win their hearts, minds, and wallets.

The affluent were never an "easy sell," but in the wake of market meltdowns and the Great Recession, gaining their trust has become even harder. "Zombie salesmanship" will no longer cut the mustard. Trust has been lost—trust in advisors, salespeople, and so-called experts. For these reasons and more, marketers and salespeople can no longer rely on the power of the company's reputation or the persuasive powers of their advertising campaigns.

Today, you must prove to each and every affluent prospect, each and every day, that your reputation is well-deserved and your advertising claims are real. You must work to build relationships with the female heads of households, as well as the males. You must nurture relationships outside of the office, and not just within. Today, selling to the affluent is about building friendships, because today's affluent trust few people beyond their friends and family—which is why throughout these chapters I'm going to use *client* rather than *customer*. When it comes to major purchase decisions, today's affluent consumer wants a consultative client relationship. They are clients, not customers.

Keep this in mind as you read the coming chapters, which I have summarized here.

Chapter 2: The Affluent Mind-Set Shift. How has the financial crisis elevated the affluent's skepticism and anxiety? How has it impacted their incomes and standards of living? This chapter answers these questions—and more. To capitalize on opportunities, salespeople must understand the lenses through which affluent consumers view the world. You'll discover their level of trust (and mistrust) in various news and advertising media. You may be shocked at how much more money they spend than the rest of the population. You'll learn about the top three criteria used by the affluent while researching purchases, as well as the top three criteria that impact their final decisions.

Chapter 3: Wowing Today's Affluent. This chapter focuses on developing loyal clients—on how to solicit repeat business and get clients to generate a buzz about your products or services. I'll also identify the top three factors impacting repeat purchases, and help you tailor an approach for each client. "Wowing" affluent clients requires highly personalized service, operational efficiency, products and services that perform exactly as promised, as well as "surprise and delight" tactics.

Chapter 4: Affluent Buzz Factor. Back in 2004, our research identified word-of-mouth as a major factor in affluent purchase decisions. Today, word-of-mouth has become *essential* to the process. By leveraging spheres of influence, you'll learn how to conduct word-of-mouth buzz campaigns. I've even included action steps to help you accelerate the buzz factor.

Chapter 5: Building Personal Relationships. Why does one BMW salesman have more repeat clients than his colleagues? How does a Nordstrom's salesman in Anchorage, Alaska, lead the whole company in sales of men's clothing? In this chapter, I'll reveal the connection between personal trust and business relationships, and discuss the inverse relationship between digital selling and affluent relationships. The more the affluent become "digitized," the more they crave personal relationships. I'll also discuss the role of social media, explaining how to use it and how *not* to use it.

Chapter 6: Creating the Right First Impression. Learn the real story of "dress for success" from the vantage point of today's affluent consumer. Among other things, I'll debunk the dress-for-success myth that originated from a 1970s bestseller. That was then; your world is now. I'll also discuss body language, eye contact, listening skills, and language skills.

Chapter 7: Today's Affluent Female. Why did the affluent female of the household return an 18-karat gold Cartier watch that her husband gave her? Why do affluent females feel awkward entering car dealerships without their husbands, even though most make the final purchase decisions? In this chapter, you'll learn dos and don'ts of communicating with the female of the household. You'll learn how to ask questions, how to proactively listen, and how to answer their questions in clear and empathetic ways.

Chapter 8: The Emerging Affluent. Although a 30-something professional earning $150,000 doesn't qualify as affluent, he represents the *emerging affluent*—a segment of the population that should not be dismissed. This demographic has real purchasing power. And because they do more online research than their older counterparts, salespeople must employ different skills to win their business. This emerging generation is price aware and value conscious, and word-of-mouth influence and two macro shifts (gender and relationship) also play a role in their financial decision making.

Chapter 9: The Amazon Effect. With each passing year, the affluent make more purchases online. Online shoppers in the United States will spend $327 billion in 2016, up 45 percent from $226 billion in 2013 and 62 percent from $202 billion in 2011.[2] In fact, most online "big ticket" purchases are made by affluent shoppers. We call this the *Amazon Effect*. Whether it's a 60-inch flat-screen LCD television, high-end luggage, clothes, jewelry, or computers, e-commerce has fundamentally changed how the affluent shop. You'll discover how affluent consumers use the Internet within the buying cycle, and what prompts them to buy one product over another.

Chapter 10: How to Move Upmarket. Our research shows a contrast between how to successfully sell to the affluent and the general population. Believe it or not, if you're able to sell to the nonaffluent, only a handful of strategic adjustments are needed to sell upmarket.

Chapter 11: Overcoming Affluent Sales Reluctance. By our definition, someone must earn at least $250,000 annually and/or have $500,000 in investable assets to qualify as affluent. Yet, most of the people who fit these definitions do *not* consider themselves affluent. Why? Because 96 percent of our affluent respondents hail from the middle class, and this has embedded middle-class mindsets and values in their subconscious.

In many respects, affluent consumers are very much like you. They work hard and value hard work in others. They're well-educated and expect their salespeople to display comparable knowledge and expertise. In this chapter, you'll learn how to recognize and overcome "social self-consciousness," a debilitating condition that holds back more salespeople than anything else.

---

[2] Sucharita Mulpuru, "U.S. Online Retail Forecast, 2011 to 2016," Forrester Research, February 27, 2012.

Chapter 12: Maximizing Your Affluent Sales Potential. I'll guide you, step-by-step, toward creating a goal-focused action plan. You'll establish sales and personal income goals, develop a daily action plan, and establish a daily reminder (trigger) to ensure execution of the daily plan. I'll also introduce (or reintroduce) you to the "achievement cycle."

Appendix: The 12 Commandments of Affluent Selling. The appendix is your "refresher course." Its 12 commandments are designed to ignite actions that will help you win over today's skeptical affluent consumers.

THE RESEARCH BEHIND THIS BOOK: 2012 AND 2013 AFFLUENT PURCHASING DECISION RESEARCH

Having studied the affluent before, during and after the Great Recession, we sought to answer one critical question, "What, if anything, has changed in how today's affluent make major investment and purchase decisions?"

This book is based largely on our 2013 Affluent Purchasing Decision (APD) Research, though a handful of data points from our Q1 2012 affluent study ($n = 400$) have also been included. The results of the 2012–2013 projects helped us identify the two macro affluent shifts and to analyze subtle changes in how the affluent approach their major financial decisions.

What makes this book so relevant, even more relevant than in 2004, is the disparity in income and spending between the affluent and the nonaffluent. Households earning $250,000 or more are spending at a rate five times greater than those earning less than $250,000. On average, the affluent have $1,362,637 in investable assets. By contrast, the rest of the nation averages $56,997 per household. This paints a clear picture of the widening gap between the haves and have nots.

However, this book isn't about income disparity or social engineering. I'll leave that to our wonderful politicians. It's a tool designed for just one purpose—to help you capitalize on the opportunities offered by today's affluent consumers.

SUMMARY

According to the Congressional Budget Office, affluent families have $28,000 more to spend per year than they did when George H.W. Bush was president. Opportunities to sell to the affluent have never been greater—for those who are prepared.

Today's affluent are a skeptical bunch who outspend the general population by five to one. Their lifestyle hasn't changed as a result of the Great Recession, but their thinking has. They've lost a lot of trust in government, experts, advertising claims, and salespeople. Our survey of households with incomes of $250,000 or more revealed that this income level marks a dividing line between the middle class and the affluent class, as well as *how* products and services must be marketed to the affluent.

Research Facts
- Affluent households earning $250,000 or more spend an average of $167,332 annually.
- The nonaffluent population averages $28,039 in annual household spending.
- The average investable assets of households earning $250,000 or more is $1,362,637.
- The average investable assets of households under $250,000 is $56,997.
- Today's affluent ranking of *personalized service* increases 22 points when respondents believe they have a personal relationship with the salesperson.
- Fifty-five percent of today's affluent have a graduate degree, compared to 12 percent of the nonaffluent.

Taking Action
- Take inventory of your current client base. Determine who meets the affluent profile and who provides you with the most business.

- Develop a plan to get to know your best clients and your potential best (those who fit the affluent profile but don't yet qualify as best clients). Include phone conversations with family members and face-to-face business and social interactions.
- Develop an action plan for getting to know the female of the household.
- Reassess your knowledge and expertise regarding the product or service that you sell.

Chapter 2 The Affluent Mind-Set Shift

Today's affluent say that advertising is the least important influence on major purchase decisions.
—Factoid, 2013 Affluent Purchasing
Decision (APD) Research

I needed a new pair of Levi's jeans—a brand I've been loyal to since college. So when my daughter mentioned a sale at the local outlet mall, I sprang into action. After donning an old pair of Levi's (to ensure I could identify the right style), I jumped in my car and drove to the store.

Although the young salesperson wasn't especially knowledgeable, she finally discovered where my style was located and directed me to a dressing room. So far, so good.

I tried on the jeans, discovered that they fit, and headed for the register. So far, so good.

I asked for confirmation of the sale price, and the young lady revealed that the discount required the purchase of *two* pairs of jeans. She even directed me to a sign advertising this caveat.

No good. In fact, this revelation was a deal-breaker.

I left without buying a thing, and later found the jeans elsewhere—for $10 less and *no* minimum purchase. For about a week, I complained about this experience to anyone who would listen. Not the kind of word-of-mouth influence salespeople like to generate.

This incident reveals not only a misunderstanding, but it also illustrates why affluent consumers have become more skeptical of advertising and salespeople.

If you were dining at a nice restaurant before the financial crisis and asked the waiter if the salmon was wild-caught or farm-raised, a cascade of events would occur. The waiter would "have to check" and your dining companions would roll their eyes and insist that you "just order the salmon; it won't kill you." Afterward, you'd spend much of the evening educating your companions on the drawbacks of farm-raised salmon.

Today, the same situation spawns an entirely different conversation. Though farm-raised salmon is still a common entrée, waitstaff have been trained to deflect the issue by saying something like, "It's been raised in the ocean in large pens outside Scotland, where the fish swim freely—almost as if they were in the wild."

What a clever response! The first time I heard this spin, I smelled a proverbial rat and repeated my question: "It is farm-raised?" The eventual reply was "Yes."

This time, my dinner companions didn't cover their faces with their menus or berate me in exasperated whispers. Instead, they silently applauded, because today's consensus is that skepticism is smart. Skepticism (even cynicism) is a reasonable response to recent revelations about seafood "mixups" in restaurants and retail markets. After I dissected the waiter's talking points, one of my friends complained about the owner of a local seafood market. Apparently, the man had been caught selling farm-raised fish as wild. And he was hardly alone:

- Scientists aiming their gene sequencers at commercial seafood are discovering rampant labeling fraud in supermarket coolers and restaurant tables: Cheap fish is often substituted for expensive fillets, and overfished species are passed off as fish whose numbers are plentiful.

- Yellowtail stands in for mahi-mahi. Nile perch is labeled as shark, and tilapia may be the Meryl Streep of seafood, capable of playing almost any role.

- Recent studies by researchers in North America and Europe harnessing the new techniques have consistently found that 20 to 25 percent of the seafood products they check are fraudulently identified, fish geneticists say.

- Labeling regulation means little if the "grouper" is really catfish or if gulf shrimp were spawned on a farm in Thailand.

- Environmentalists, scientists, and foodies are complaining that regulators are lax in policing seafood, and have been slow to adopt the latest scientific tools even though they are now readily available and easy to use. "Customers buying fish have a right to know what the heck it is and where it's from, but agencies like the FDA are not taking this as seriously as they should," said Michael Hirschfield, chief scientist of the nonprofit group Oceana, referring to the Food and Drug Administration.[1]

---

[1] Elisabeth Rosenthal, "Tests Reveal Mislabeling of Fish," *New York Times*, May 26, 2011.

Those poor tilapia and farm-raised salmon. . . . This isn't about them. It's about the mind-set of today's merchants and salespeople and the justifiable reactions of affluent consumers.

The affluent have become jaded for good reason, which is why they no longer hesitate to ask tough questions of potential vendors. No longer will they accept whatever canned response they receive. Their "BS antennae" are fully extended at all times.

Whether it's the food they eat, the clothes they buy, or the luxury cruises they take, ad campaigns have very little impact on the affluent final decision. Advertising helps in name recognition, but today's affluent don't believe advertising claims any more. In fact, they often take delight in deconstructing and debunking the claims. Remember, the affluent are the most highly educated people in America. They didn't become prosperous by being naïve, poorly informed, or stupid.

Let's examine affluent *trust* using empirical data gathered from our latest APD survey. The following chart represents trust in advertising. A positive response (trust factor) required the respondent to have "some to full trust" in the surveyed industry or profession.

Trust in Advertising (Trust Factor)

Computer companies	52%
Banks	49%
Food/beverage companies	49%
Financial advisors	44%
Drug companies	44%
Automotive industry	42%
Insurance firms	40%
Cell phone companies	40%

These stats may not seem especially devastating, but let's put them in perspective: Would you retain a lawyer, pharmacist, family physician, or financial advisor whom you trusted less than half the time? Would you submit to voluntary surgery or hire a building contractor if you believed the odds of a successful outcome were less than 50 percent?

I hope not. You can get better odds in a game of blackjack.

According to Kantar Media, the automotive industry devoted $13.9 billion to advertising in 2011.[2] GM alone spent $1.78 billion. How can an industry spend that much to reach affluent consumers, and generate a trust factor of only 42 percent? What's gone wrong?

For one thing, I can't help but laugh when I see many car commercials.

Not long ago, I was facilitating an affluent round-table discussion at a sports bar when the topic of advertising was broached. In the midst of the discussion, a car commercial aired—one featuring basketball superstar Shaquille O'Neal, who was pitching a new Buick.

"You never see him *getting* into the car," said one observer.

"Look at his knees!" said another. "They're touching the dashboard."

"*Nobody* could fit in that back seat," said the first person.

"These ads are unbelievable," added a third person. "Do they expect us to believe that Shaq—all seven-foot-one and 390 pounds of him—is actually *driving* that car?"

So much for truth in advertising.

This type of pitch doesn't fly with today's affluent shoppers, regardless of how much the company spends on the ad campaign. Perhaps this explains why only 42 percent of the affluent have any trust in automotive advertising. And drug companies aren't faring much better. According to Kantar Media, Pfizer spent $1.2 billion on advertising in 2011 to generate an unimpressive 44 percent trust factor among the affluent. I don't know about you, but when a pharmaceutical ad features 40 seconds of disclaimers about the drug's side effects for every 20 seconds devoted to benefits, I'm inclined to pass on that "miracle product."

---

[2] "Kantar Media Reports U.S. Advertising Expenditures Increased 0.8 Percent in 2011," Kantar Media, March 12, 2012.

Meanwhile, Verizon spent $1.64 billion and AT&T spent $1.9 billion during the same period to generate a mere 40 percent trust factor among the affluent. Ouch.

Madison Avenue, Wall Street, Detroit, and the rest of the corporate world haven't yet figured out how to influence affluent consumers. If you listen to advertising "experts," you'll hear lots of talk about mobile ads, and how "new media" will soon supplant TV and print advertising for the lion's share of advertising dollars.

Really? Do they *really* think mobile ads are the answer? Do they really believe that smart and skeptical shoppers will trust (much less appreciate) a perpetual stream of ads pumped onto their smartphones? Our research indicates that they won't. It tells us that selling to the affluent requires that you build personal relationships with them—that you first build trust.

As I was airing these thoughts with a colleague, he responded with a story of his own. "My Time Warner cable bill kept going up and up. We weren't watching much television, so I called to cancel the service. The rep immediately offered to cut my bill in half.

"I was so annoyed that I tweeted my experience and got more responses than I cared to track from people sharing similar stories." (Note: I should mention that this colleague is a nationally recognized social media guru.) "And after my wife told the story to two colleagues, both of them dropped Time Warner and switched to the service we'd decided to use."

In one of those "Ah-ha!" moments, he concluded: "It really is about personal interaction, trusted relationships, and word-of-mouth influence."

PRE- AND POSTCRISIS DECISION MAKING

What's remained constant between the precrisis affluent of and today's affluent is that there's never enough time in the day to accomplish everything. Hence, whenever the affluent make a major purchase decision, they want honest and personalized assistance. Compare the seven factors that drive affluent purchase decisions—*before* and *after* the financial crisis:

1. **Precrisis:** They want to be respected (even honored) for the level of success they've achieved.

   Postcrisis: They want to develop a relationship built on trust *before* making a major financial decision.

2. **Precrisis:** They've succeeded because of their professionalism and competence, and expect the same from others.

   Postcrisis: No change.

3. **Precrisis:** They react to perceived deception and manipulation by taking their business elsewhere.

   Postcrisis: They're on high alert for signs of deceit and manipulation. Whenever these are detected, they not only take their business elsewhere, but embark on negative word-of-mouth campaigns.

4. **Precrisis:** They define value on their own terms, based on research. Then they do whatever it takes to obtain value, even if it means buying from websites or warehouse clubs.

   Postcrisis: They continue to perform research, but rely more heavily on the opinions and recommendations of people they trust and respect. Skepticism has elevated the power of word-of-mouth influence in their major purchase decisions.

5. **Precrisis:** Instead of striving to keep up with the Joneses, they want to be different from the Joneses.

   Postcrisis: They aren't focused on the Joneses at all. They're focused on work and family.

6. **Precrisis:** They experience enough tension and hassles in their daily life. They want to be free from that when dealing with people who want to sell them something.

   Postcrisis: They have resigned themselves to a "lack of truth in advertising" and expect unforeseen hassles when making major purchases. They want products and services to deliver as promised, or better.

7. **Precrisis:** They are willing to pay for the best information, the best products, the highest level of competence, and the best professional service.

   Postcrisis: Although they can afford to pay for the best of everything, they are more price conscious and warranty conscious.

If there's a single unifying theme to these post-crisis purchase criteria, it's *trust*. Today's affluent have money to spend, but they are more guarded. Convincing them to buy requires a higher level of sales skill, and requires that products/services meet or exceed their expectations.

PRE- AND POSTCRISIS LIFESTYLES

There are many sources of data describing how the financial crisis affected different population segments. To obtain specifics on how the affluent fared, and compare them with the rest of the population, we chose two metrics: (1) changes to income/job status, and (2) changes to standards of living. The results were unexpected: 81 percent of affluent respondents (male and female) described no change or a positive change to their income/job status. By contrast, 51 percent of the nonaffluent said the same. Our findings on standards of living were comparable: 84 percent of affluent men and 79 percent of affluent women are enjoying a lifestyle that is unchanged or even better.

Income/Job Status

	Nonaffluent		Affluent	
	Men	Women	Men	Women
Much worse	33%	21%	3%	6%
Slightly worse	16%	24%	15%	14%
Neutral	36%	39%	30%	46%
Better	15%	16%	51%	35%

Standard of Living

	Nonaffluent		Affluent	
	Men	Women	Men	Women
Much worse	31%	18%	2%	5%
Slightly worse	27%	27%	14%	16%
Neutral	26%	42%	33%	49%
Better	15%	13%	51%	30%

SUMMARY

Today's affluent are working hard, and a significant number are improving their lifestyles. However, they don't consider themselves wealthy, so don't call them that to their faces. They want personalized service and expect their major purchases to perform as advertised.

Their distrust in advertising can be turned into an advantage for the salesperson who masters the art of building long-term trust. Few salespeople have this level of skill, but this knowledge is available to anyone who will take the time to master what is presented in the following chapters. Remember: Selling to the affluent can be *your* ticket to affluence.

Research Facts

- Ninety-four percent of affluent men are currently in the workforce.
- Ninety-one percent of affluent women are currently in the workforce.
- Eighty-one percent of affluent (male and female) claim their income status has either improved or remained unchanged since the financial crisis.
- Eighty-four percent of affluent men and 79 percent of affluent women say their lifestyles have either improved or remained unchanged since the financial crisis.

- Affluent trust in advertising is below 50 percent for banks, food/beverage companies, drug companies, the automotive industry, insurance firms, and cell phone companies.
- The automotive industry spent $13.9 billion on advertising in 2011, according to Kantar Media's 2011 statistics.

Taking Action
- Understand your products and services backward and forward.
- Be aware of all advertising promises.
- Be sure every feature and benefit is delivered *exactly* as advertised and is clearly understood in advance by clients/customers.
- Develop a more personal relationship with your customers by asking personal questions related to your products and services.
- Don't patronize affluent clients, and do *not* refer to them as affluent, wealthy, or rich.

Chapter 3 Wowing Today's Affluent

Ninety-five percent of today's affluent cite previous good service as the number one factor in making a repeat purchase.

—Factoid, 2013 APD Research

Imagine an abandoned Exxon station on the edge of a wealthy neighborhood, fronting a busy four-lane road. Now imagine this same gas station bustling with predominately affluent clients. One mile from my office in Greensboro, North Carolina, this is the reality. Less than three months after the station was purchased by Gaurav Patel, it was transformed from eyesore to *wow* store. In fact, Patel created such a buzz in the neighborhood that he generated a front-page story in our daily newspaper: "Station pumps gas, cleans windows—free!"

If purchasing gasoline can be turned into an affluent wow experience, you have no excuse for failing to wow your affluent clients. I interviewed Patel to see how he worked his miracle:

After buying the vacant station, Patel implemented a simple idea he'd been formulating for a while: providing extraordinary service. The "package" includes complimentary pump service (something that largely disappeared from gas stations in the late 1970s) and windshield cleaning for every client from 10 A.M. to 6 P.M., Monday through Friday. The air pressure in your tires is checked and filled as needed. Dogs get biscuits, kids get lollipops, and names are remembered. Visiting the station is like entering a scene in the movie *American Graffiti*. And it was all made possible by a young man earning his psychology degree at night—someone Patel hired to help him transform gasoline purchases into wow experiences.

It wasn't long before the buzz about this new business traveled through this affluent neighborhood, a blend of upscale professionals and retirees, old money and new. Initially, people were shocked. They couldn't believe someone was pumping gas again. But soon, word-of-mouth influence began spreading with the speed of a brush fire.

During my interview with Patel, he said with pride, "I just got a call from a lady who was driving back to Virginia. She thanked me for such a wonderful experience."

Someone from another state phones a gas station from the highway to say thank you? That earns a big-time *wow*!

"Sixty percent of my customers are women," Patel continued. "They love the service, and many will drive clear across town to buy gas from me."

Of course, the real money is made inside the small shop, where Patel sells the standard fare: lottery tickets and soft drinks. He also stocks quality wines for the affluent neighbors who want quick but personalized service. During my last visit, one customer asked Patel about a set of expensive headphones on display near the register. A few minutes later, the customer bought them with Patel's promise, "If you don't like them, you can always bring them back."

The secret to Patel's success is differentiation through personalized service. Never underestimate the importance of personal service and the power of affluent buzz.

When was the last time you enjoyed extraordinary service? You might have to think for a while, but I'm sure you can remember. Was it at a restaurant, a luxury hotel, or an auto dealership? Wherever it occurred, odds are good that once wowed, you talked about the experience with coworkers, friends, family, and neighbors—anyone who would listen.

Unfortunately, service today is often so shoddy that a good experience is the exception instead of the rule, which is why we're so wowed whenever we enjoy an outstanding experience.

YOUR "WOW" SERVICE EXPERIENCE

To deliver exceptional service, think from the perspective of your clients. Can they tell you're prepared for your meetings? Do they get the impression you've made the investment of time, energy, and resources to provide service beyond what's expected? Is their face-to-face experience with you memorable? How do they receive follow-up? Do they receive a letter, an email, or a card? Do they get the perception that you go above and beyond the mundane? These questions and more need to be asked and answered.

The following are five simple action steps that can assist you in this endeavor:

1. Make a list of your affluent and/or best clients.
2. Assess your next face-to-face encounters with these clients.
3. Determine the actions you could take (fine tuning) to make the first face-to-face encounter more of a "wow" experience.
4. Decide how you will follow up after each face-to-face encounter.
5. Devise a plan to gather as much personal information as you can about these top clients.

The basic premise here is actually quite simple: Analyze your current service model and commit to taking it to the next level.

SURPRISE AND DELIGHT: A SIMPLE WAY TO WOW AFFLUENT CLIENTS

The fact that your product or service will perform as advertised should be a given. This is a bare-minimum expectation among the affluent. It's why they're willing to pay a premium price, but it's a wow factor that converts skeptical prospects into loyal clients. Although good service is now a rarity, affluent salespeople must be better than good. They must master the art of surprise and delight.

The old adage that it costs less to keep existing clients than find new ones is only part of the story. The other part is the wellspring of new business opportunities you can produce by surprising and delighting affluent clients.

You can launch this process by thinking in terms of coffee table books. When you're interacting with a client, ask yourself, "What coffee table book would I send to this client?" This doesn't mean you have to send an actual coffee table book. The question is merely a reminder to gather enough personal information to discern the person's interests and passions.

What does surprise and delight mean?

- *Surprise:* The client is surprised that you were *really* listening— that you know he or she is about to experience a major life event or is passionate about music, baseball, dogs, and so on.
- *Delight:* The client is delighted that you gave them such a thoughtful gift.

THE LAW OF RECIPROCITY

This concept was popularized by Dr. Robert Cialdini in his best-selling book *Influence: The Psychology of Persuasion.*[1] His premise: When you give someone a gift, even if it's not wanted, the recipient feels obligated to return the favor. This means that whenever you go the extra mile for affluent clients, they will find a way to return the gesture.

Surprise and delight consists of nothing more than delivering a nice, thoughtful gift. Your clients will be impressed (wowed), and some will provide immediate return favors in the form of introductions and referrals. Over time, others will stimulate positive word-of-mouth influence on your behalf.

If you're wondering how to wow the wealthy client who has everything, the answer is personally and creatively.

Louis, an interior decorator on the West Coast, offers a good example. He plies his craft in a world of multimillion-dollar estates. His clients insist on the best furnishings, and usually want everything show-and-tell ready when they're ready to entertain. Because they spend small fortunes on the interiors of their homes, the competition among decorators is fierce.

---

[1] Robert Cialdini, *Influence: The Psychology of Persuasion* (New York: HarperBusiness, 2006).

Because decorating is such a personal process, everyone in the field has an advantage when it comes to intelligence gathering. However, Louis is a master. He might not be *the* best interior decorator, but he's by far the best marketer. His chief weapon is surprising and delighting his clients *months* after the work is completed.

One wealthy client owns a Chihuahua who "loves me more than my wife." This is a household joke, because his wife refuses to travel to their condo in Hawaii. Therefore, Mickey (the Chihuahua) substitutes as his traveling companion on first-class flights to the islands.

In the spirit of "personal and creative," Louis photographed Mickey dressed in his travel sweater before one flight. Then, while Mickey and Dad were in Hawaii, Louis had the photo framed and engraved. It was delivered three days after the vacationers returned from the trip.

Said Louis: "The surprise and delight reaction was off the charts. It was all he could talk about. This simple personal gift was directly responsible for over $250,000 of business."

Mickey's dad activated a serious word-of-mouth campaign. He became Louis's advocate. Not only did he personally introduce Louis to everyone in his wealthy spheres of influence, but whenever any type of décor discussion occurred, he strongly recommended Louis as the best person for the job.

Granted, not every surprise and delight initiative will hit the jackpot, but it *will* have a positive impact and accelerate your affluent sales. Louis attributes serious dollars to one wow experience. Patel attributes *all* of his success to transforming commodity products into personal experiences. Any way you look at it, wowing today's affluent is good business.

When you truly wow an affluent client, you activate what we call the *Relationship Management/Relationship Marketing Nexus*™. You strengthen the current relationship and activate positive word-of-mouth influence—the heart and soul of relationship marketing.

Since most of you aren't interior decorators, let's examine ways to gather the intelligence needed for surprise and delight.

UNCOVERING CLIENT INFORMATION

We've discovered that those who enjoy the most success in affluent sales have mastered the art of gathering personal information from clients and prospects. There are three reasons why the task of personal intelligence gathering is so critical:

1. It strengthens the loyalty of affluent clients.
2. It increases the probability of further monetizing the relationship (future sales) by helping you personalize your services to create wow experiences.
3. It activates positive word-of-mouth influence, increasing referrals and introductions.

To gather intelligence, ask questions in a conversational manner and really listen to the answers. This can be accomplished by following these three simple rules:

- Talk 20 percent of the time and spend the rest listening.
- Help clients help *you* by asking specific questions about their favorite subject: themselves.
- Note special events and passions (Mickey's trips to Hawaii) and document them.

Surprise and Delight: Quick Tips
- Be personal—think "coffee table book."
- Link the gift to a special event—Mickey's trip to Hawaii.
- Think inexpensive—the framed and engraved photo cost less than $100.
- Employ irregular timing—the degree of irregularity is directly proportional to the degree of surprise. An annual birthday gift might be appreciated, but isn't much of a surprise.
- Remember the 80/20 rule—most companies devote 80 percent of their marketing dollars to finding new clients and 20 percent

to servicing current clients. *You* will do the opposite. Spending money on your current clients, in thoughtful ways, strengthens the relationships and stimulates positive word-of-mouth influence.

- Use alternative intelligence gathering methods—Google search, Facebook, and a LinkedIn profile can uncover a wealth of information.
- Choose gifts with a lasting impact—Mickey's framed picture will last longer than a bottle of wine or a bouquet of flowers.

Next I discuss some surprise and delight ideas that have been used to great effect.

Major Life Events

Keep your eyes and ears open for major life events—the marriage of a child, a seminal wedding anniversary, birth of a grandchild, graduations, and so forth. Yes, gifts delivered at these times *are* expected, but they aren't necessarily expected from service providers. This presents a terrific opportunity to distinguish yourself from your competitors. Also, these gestures tend to generate invitations to the actual events. Don't forget to learn where children attend kindergarten, high school, and college, when they're scheduled to graduate, and whether they have plans to celebrate the events.

Vacations

In addition to spending more money on vacations than the nonaffluent, the affluent also take more vacations, which is why these events are a great time to enhance relationships. Whether the client is taking an international vacation or a family trip to a national park, send a thoughtful gift that enhances the experience—a Rick Steves travel guide about a European destination or Ken Burns's book on the national parks. These gifts often stimulate positive word-of-mouth influence.

The Right Gifts

A small package was waiting on my desk when I returned from summer vacation. When I opened it, I discovered (to my surprise and delight) a pair of cufflinks made from the links of a bicycle chain. A note read: "I loved your lecture on the affluent and I was listening—hope you enjoy the cufflinks, as I know you're a cyclist." A business card was also included.

I emailed my thanks, as well as a handwritten note, and placed the business card in my wallet as a reminder. That simple gesture illustrates the value of selecting the right gift. I love to cycle, and often make reference to that fact during my lectures. And since French cuffs are my standard fare, a pair of cycling cufflinks hit the mark.

When it comes to gifts, it's vital to think in terms of personal *passion points*. Books are an excellent gift if you know your client is a reader. However, sending a novel to someone who reads business books isn't appropriate. Be sure to gather intelligence before selecting the gift.

Personalized products for pets are another hot gift category. Many affluent pamper their pets even more than their children. Among the affluent, there are more dogs, cats, ferrets, and fish that enjoy Mickey's exalted status than you probably realize.

Before we move on, here are a few more special gifts that tend to active the wow factor:

- Wine (specific to their tastes)
- Books (linked to their interests)
- Flowers
- Edible gift baskets
- Magazine subscriptions
- Health and beauty gift baskets
- Cigars
- Inscribed items (adding a personalized inscription to an item matching the client's passion)
- Chocolates
- Charitable donations

- College care packages
- Personalized luggage tags
- Tickets to a sporting or cultural event
- Crystal
- Gardening products

Since your mission is to make wowing a regular part of your routine, we recommend that "surprise and delight" be an agenda item as you plan each upcoming week. This doesn't mean you should send gifts on a weekly basis. The objective is to remind yourself to gather intelligence—the kind you need to select perfect gifts in the near future. You should always be thinking about the perfect "coffee table book" when interacting with the affluent.

Following is the form we give coaching clients to help them improve their intelligence-gathering efforts.

Client Information Tracker

Basic Information

Name
Marital status
Spouse's name
Home address
Vacation home address
Wedding anniversary
Hometown (both spouses)
Birth date (both spouses)
College/graduate school (both spouses)
Military service (both spouses)

Communication

Business phone (both spouses)
Home phone
Cell phone (both spouses)

Fax
Email (both spouses)
Website
Social media: Facebook, LinkedIn, Twitter, and so on (both spouses)

Business/Employment

Business (both spouses)
Business address (both spouses)
Position (both spouses)
Previous employment (both spouses)

Children

Name, age, school status, marital status, and so on

Grandchildren

Number of grandchildren (names, ages, and so on)

Personal

Health issues and history
Community activities
Political activities
Religious activities
Service organizations
Favorite restaurants
Hobbies/recreational interests
Vacation habits
Cars
Conversational interests and habits
Close friends
Close family
Other

Service That Goes Beyond Expectations

It's not all about buying the right gift. Many times, you'll be able to wow a client through above-and-beyond service. Recently, a bicycle shop employee drove to Mrs. Affluent's house to help change a flat tire on her $2,500 bike. He also brought with him an easy-to-manage bike rack that fits on most car trunks. After changing the tire, he demonstrated how the rack worked, fitted the straps to Mrs. Affluent's Mercedes, and helped her practice getting the bike on and off the rack. He then explained that if she liked the rack, he'd leave it with her. She could pay for it the next time she stopped by the shop. Not only did Mrs. Affluent purchase the bike rack, she steered two friends to the store to purchase bikes.

A wealthy widow, four months removed from the death of her husband, had neglected her yard to the extent that the overzealous homeowners association sent her a warning letter. Distraught, she called one of her husband's three financial advisors who lived in the neighborhood. The next day, the advisor's lawn service sent a crew of four to turn her yard into a showcase. It cost the advisor $800. He did it because it was the right thing to do, and now he's the only financial advisor handling this wealthy widow's financial affairs.

SUMMARY

Providing good service is no longer good enough in light of the Amazon Effect. Wowing today's affluent requires attention to detail, personal interaction, and many small touches. Think of this chapter as a guide and a call to action—one that encourages you to initiate the *wowing* process. Shower affluent clients with love and attention and, in turn, they will shower you with praise, introduce you to friends, and provide a constant stream of referrals.

Research Facts
- Personalizing a business relationship strengthens loyalty.
- Ninety-five percent of affluent consumers cite good service as the number one criterion for repeat business (loyalty).

- Personalized service is essential to good service.
- Personal service that goes beyond the expected creates a wow experience.
- Products and services that perform as expected don't wow the affluent.
- Gathering personal information is the key to wowing and wooing upscale clients.

Taking Action
- Profile each affluent client to determine the extent of the personal information you already have on each family.
- Develop a systematic process for gathering personal information on each affluent client.
- Initiate a surprise and delight campaign targeting affluent clients.
- Think of surprise and delight opportunities at the beginning of each week.
- Commit to at least one "surprise and delight" a year for every affluent client.
- Execute one personal service experience that goes beyond the expected.
- Commit to one act of kindness a day.

Chapter 4   Affluent Buzz Factor

*Hosting a fun event for affluent clients and guests cre-
ates the most immediate buzz because it is most likely
to be attended and enjoyed by everyone.*
                    —Factoid, 2013 APD Research

Let's be crystal clear: If Patel can create buzz in affluent circles with the service station described in Chapter 3, *everyone* is capable of activating affluent buzz.

What's the difference between wowing affluent clients and starting a buzz? They're so closely connected that one contributes to the other. Wowing creates buzz. When you surprise and delight an affluent client, the law of reciprocity is activated and good things usually happen. The same is true when you deliver service that goes beyond the expected. Positive word-of-mouth begins, but these conversations occur after the fact—after something triggers a reminder.

Assuming you're now wowing affluent clients, the question becomes how do you trigger a reminder? The secret to getting clients talking is giving them something to talk about.

To help you generate more buzz, I've constructed this chapter around three interrelated methodologies:

1. *Intimate events.* These enable you to get social with affluent clients and penetrate their spheres of influence.
2. A *visibility campaign.* This gets you involved in the community, socially or civically, ensuring you are seen with the right people in the right environments.
3. *Social media.* This magnifies and disseminates the buzz.

If Patel wanted to take the affluent buzz he's already activated to the next level, these three methodologies would serve him well. He could set aside one Saturday a month for a face-painting event for the children and grandchildren of his best clients. He could hand out flyers while people are getting gas, or send email reminders as announcements—all of which would reinforce the buzz. With a digital camera and Facebook, Patel could memorialize his face-painting event. People love pictures of their children and grandchildren. You can probably imagine the ongoing buzz he would generate as his best clients posted photos taken at the service station of their children showing off their little painted faces.

Patel's service station could also sponsor the local girls' soccer team, supplying them with T-shirts that promote his business. This would create more visibility for the business, helping to maintain the buzz within his affluent client's spheres of influence.

Let's examine spheres of influence. The typical affluent family has seven:

1. Family members: siblings, cousins, parents, adult children, etcetera
2. Recreation: golf, tennis, walking, cycling, bridge, cooking, etcetera
3. Colleagues: associates, partners, managers, etcetera
4. Organizations: civic, religious, boards, etcetera
5. Neighbors
6. Professionals: doctor, dentist, attorney, CPA, etcetera
7. Friends

Your mission is to uncover the names of people in each of these seven spheres. Granted, not everyone will know affluent prospects that need your products or services. However, the process will

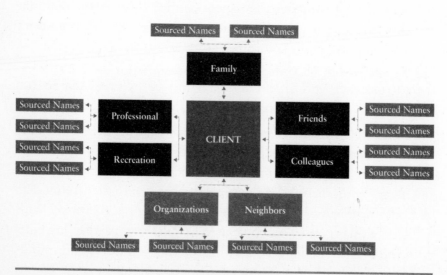

FIGURE 4.1   The Seven Affluent Spheres of Influence

help to stimulate buzz within the world of each affluent client. You will unleash a domino effect as, person by person, you create a buzz within each contact's seven spheres.

We use the model in Figure 4.1 in our affluent sales coaching. It serves as a reminder to always keep your antenna activated when it comes to uncovering the names of people within clients' spheres of influence. You might want to make a copy as a reminder to do the same.

HOSTING AN INTIMATE CLIENT EVENT

As I was writing this chapter, Kevin, who oversees all of our affluent sales coaches, shared the story of two financial planners he was personally coaching. They zeroed in on their clients' passion for cars by hosting an auto-themed event that generated serious buzz.

These financial planners were both self-proclaimed "flash car buffs." One owned a Ferrari, and the other owned an Aston Martin. In one coaching session, they mentioned that many of their affluent clients were also car enthusiasts. Soon, the discussion turned to hosting an intimate event based on exotic cars.

Their first step was identifying clients who were genuine car enthusiasts. Each advisor had about 15 clients in his "recreational sphere of influence" who fit this profile. Next, Kevin instructed them to ask each of these clients to identify friends who shared this passion. It was the proverbial "birds of a feather flock together" approach—and it worked. Within two weeks, the financial planners compiled a list of more than 70 car enthusiasts.

Up next was devising a fun and creative event to host. In response to that challenge, one of the financial advisors came up with a great idea: partnering with an exotic automobile dealership, which could cohost the event at their facility. They selected a local McLaren dealership, met with the general manager, and sold him on the idea. It wasn't exactly a hard sell—not after the men mentioned that a couple dozen wealthy car enthusiasts would be attending.

Next, they selected a date on which the dealership would close the showroom to everyone but the invited guests and provide wine and hors d'oeuvres. Together, the dealership's GM and the financial planners (I'll call them Wow and Buzz) determined that 20 people—clients and guests—would be the perfect number for the "wow" event.

Wow and Buzz then telephoned five of their wealthy clients, and sold them on the event, suggesting that each bring as a guest another car enthusiast friend (they'd already sourced names using the spheres-of-influence model). To their pleasant surprise, the buzz ignited the moment the invitations were extended.

The event went off without a hitch. Everyone enjoyed himself, and nobody abused the wine before driving the cars. The entire focus was on these expensive automobiles. More important, Wow and Buzz were able to strengthen the loyalty of their wealthy clients and forge relationships with the guests who attended the event.

The "buzz factor" was immediate, traveling in a number of directions. Within two days, the owner of the dealership invited Wow and Buzz to lunch at his club, asking to schedule another event and inquiring if they could also review the dealership's 401(k) plan. A few days later, a guest at the event became a client. And the "buzz factor" had just begun.

What's important to understand with the buzz factor is that it is *not* product-driven or dependent on affluent sales skills. As a cruise line, you don't generate buzz because the luxury cruise you sold was truly a luxury cruise. So too, Wow and Buzz won't get a lot (if any) positive word-of-mouth influence for their financial planning skills. The buzz factor is activated when the salesperson goes above and beyond expectations in more personal ways.

REASONS TO AVOID LARGE-SCALE CLIENT EVENTS

Much has been written about conducting client events, but the focus is often on larger events. Here are five reasons to avoid these larger-scale client events (often labeled *client appreciation events*):

1. They aren't exclusive to affluent clients. They tend to be large affairs, with every client and prospect receiving an emailed invitation. As a result, few if any affluent clients attend. Today's affluent want exclusivity; they want to feel special.

2. They aren't personal. The invitation isn't personal and the event isn't personal; therefore, they generate little if any buzz among the affluent. Personal interaction amplifies the buzz.

3. Large client events are expensive and require more effort. Keep in mind that you'll be hosting a huge party, inviting everyone you've ever met (most of whom you don't know and won't recognize), and overseeing all the logistics required to pull it off.

4. Large client events involve little to no relationship marketing. This is ironic, given the time, effort, and expense associated with large-scale client events. Smaller, intimate client events are usually more productive. They are the number one event that affluent clients want to attend, the event to which they'll want to bring a guest, and the type of event most highly prized by targeted prospects.

5. Large client events are held infrequently, usually once a year. Unless you're hosting a private concert with the Rolling Stones, the buzz factor will need to be constantly reinforced. Affluent buzz needs constant massage to stay alive.

We live in a new world. The large client event of yesteryear served its purpose. Salespeople got in front of large groups with the hope of cementing loyalty and obtaining additional business.

During a recent affluent research project, we formulated a question about intimate client events hosted by financial advisors. When we asked "Which of the following events hosted by your financial advisor would you rather attend?" we received the responses seen in Figure 4.2. Note that large-scale events scored dead last, whereas small-scale social events ranked first.

Today's affluent consumers want you to give them reasons to activate a buzz.

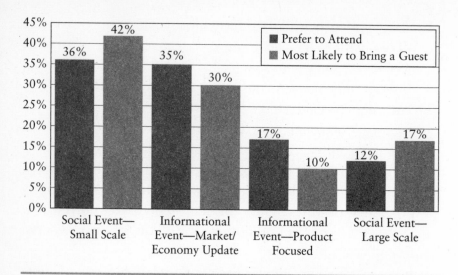

FIGURE 4.2   Affluent Investor Perception of Client Events

THREE OBJECTIVES

The real beauty of intimate client events is that they enable you to fully activate the Relationship Management/Relationship Marketing Nexus™. First and foremost, they help you build on existing relationships and strengthen the loyalty of your best clients. You've expressed your appreciation through your actions. Second, you create a safe nonsales environment for your top clients, encouraging them to personally introduce you to people in their spheres of influence, which enables you to expand your network. Third, you instantly activate the buzz factor before, during, and after the event among both clients and prospects.

1. *Expressing appreciation*

   By now, it should come as no surprise that a key ingredient of attracting and developing loyal affluent clients is the depth of the relationships you build with them. Large client-appreciation events, product-specific seminars, and the like don't achieve this objective. Intimate client events do. These events are all about relationships. They create a safe environment in which personal interactions flourish. You and your clients will see each other in a more relaxed and informal setting—one in which you interact at a more personal level as you enjoy the experiences together.

2. *Expanding your network*

One of the biggest benefits of strengthening loyalty is the personal introductions and referrals (solicited and unsolicited) you'll receive from your clients. And these referrals are usually affluent consumers with similar resources and needs. Because word-of-mouth influence plays a major role in the major purchase decisions of today's affluent, strategically crafted intimate events are an ideal platform for activating this form of influence. You always want to encourage clients to bring guests, preferably couples or individuals you have sourced from their spheres of influence. Why? Because the odds are high that these prospects will be a lot like your existing clients in terms of their tastes and temperaments. *Note:* It's important to emphasize to affluent clients that no business will be discussed during the events. The only purpose is fun.

3. *Activating your buzz factor*

Your buzz factor will be activated as a direct result of your intimate event. However, the timing of the buzz will depend on the event. In the case of Wow and Buzz, the McLaren event generated a buzz before the event, intensified during the event, and accelerated afterward. Not only did it spread through networks of affluent clients, but also through luxury car dealerships. Because Wow and Buzz initially identified over 70 clients and prospects for the event, they can maintain the buzz by scheduling another luxury car event. When I discuss social media later in this chapter, I'll share exactly how they were able to spread the buzz.

It's important to understand that the guests invited by your clients should be viewed as *potential prospects*, not prospective clients.

Your purpose is to socialize with them and demonstrate how you express appreciation to your valued clients, even if you know that some of these people are interested in your product or services.

It's through events like these that you establish the trust and credibility that becomes the heart and soul of your affluent buzz factor. Wow and Buzz's clients and guests were raving about the event, but woven throughout that buzz was the implicit professionalism and credibility of Buzz and Wow. This is what makes you magnetic. The buzz factor attracts the right people. If guests enjoy your event, you will have made a strong favorable impression with clients and potential prospects.

So how do you conduct intimate events that activate the Relationship Management/Relationship Marketing Nexus™? Here are five steps to help maximize the value of these events.

FIVE STEPS TO ACTIVATE AFFLUENT BUZZ VIA INTIMATE EVENTS

Step 1: Select the Right Clients

First, identify the clients you'd like to invite to an event. Too many salespeople make the mistake of skipping this step. Instead, they selected an event and a date that works for them, without even thinking of their clients. Not so fast! Intimate client events should be built around your clients and *their* likes, so your first step is identifying which people fit your affluent client profile. To maximize the buzz factor of your initial events, select people who are likely to bring well-qualified guests. You want these events to build momentum, so encourage everyone to bring guests. As you develop your list of affluent clients, search for their common passions, interests, and hobbies.

Step 2: Create the Right Event

Let's review what prompted Buzz and Wow to create a luxury car event. They had a number of affluent clients who, like them, were car enthusiasts, and they knew these clients had affluent friends who shared that passion. During a coaching session with Kevin, they brainstormed how to tie this interest to an event. The result was a smashing success. Had they copped out and settled for, say, a generic dinner hosted by their firm, they might have had trouble getting clients to attend, much less bring guests.

We're often asked which types of event are best. Our response: It depends on your clientele. Don't think you need to hold a luxury car event. In fact, as much as Buzz and Wow loved cars, they never considered such an event until the sales coach walked them through this process. That said, here are a few ideas to jump-start your imagination:

- Life milestone events: Birthdays, anniversaries, and graduations are excellent opportunities to honor clients and their family members.
- Cultural events: Art exhibits, concerts, theater outings, and events honoring the culture of the community.
- Entertainment: Tap the interests of key clients, whether it's wine, cars, cooking, antiques, gardening, or playing bridge.
- Sporting events: Whether as observers or participants, golf, tennis, softball, and boating are crowd pleasers. Tickets to college and professional sporting events are also appreciated by fans of the local teams.
- Educational events: Inviting clients to hear a well-known speaker is one option. Another is booking a speaker to discuss a topic of keen interest to a select group of clients and their guests. Many speakers will do this free of charge to promote their businesses.
- Charitable events: Select with care, knowing that your clients will be solicited by the organization sponsoring the event. Helping your clients meet potential prospects for their businesses could be one reason to invite them, but it's important to make sure the right people attend.

Specific Intimate Event Ideas
- Barbecues
- Sporting events

- Cooking classes
- Golf clinics
- Art gallery tours
- Private museum tours
- Chocolate tastings
- Luxury car events
- Theater night
- Gardening events
- Flower arranging class
- Pet event (dogs)
- Tailgating
- Spa day
- Ballroom dance classes

Step 3: Master the Invitation Process

The invitation is arguably the most critical part of stimulating affluent buzz around intimate client events. Inviting the right people catalyzes the process, enabling you to maximize your buzz. The following are three simple steps for issuing effective invitations:

1. *The initial call.* Your invitation needs to be made over the telephone or in person. You are personally selling the event, and your enthusiasm and descriptions are what activate the buzz factor and increase attendance. You can send a written invitation as a secondary point of contact, but the initial invitation should be done by the salesperson. Remember, this is a part of your relationship-management strategy, so make it *personal*. Key points to stress in the invitation are:
   - This is all fun; no business! This is where you sell your event.
   - Everyone is bringing a guest (if possible, mention a specific guest you'd like them to bring).
   - You're inviting only an intimate group of your best and most beloved clients.

- You will be calling back to confirm their attendance and that of their guest.

The following script was used by Buzz and Wow. We use variations on this same theme, making slight adjustments depending on the type of event.

> Buzz: Mr. Client, Wow and I are going to be hosting a car event for a small group of our car enthusiast clients, like you, at the McLaren dealership on October 15th at 7 P.M. Have you ever driven a McLaren? The dealership is closing, providing wine and hors-d'oeuvres, and the place will be all ours—it's going to be a blast! All fun— no business. Why don't you bring your colleague Bobby as a guest? You said Bobby was a car guy—he's going to love driving a McLaren.
>
> Mr. Client: Sounds great. I'm already pumped. Let me check with Bobby.
>
> Buzz: Great. It's going to be a blast. I've always wanted to drive a McLaren. I'll be finalizing our guest list Friday, so I'll circle back with you to see if Bobby can make it. Hope he can. He's going to love it.

2. *Confirmation/invitation note.* To those who accept your invitation, mail a written confirmation of the event that includes the location, directions, and parking details. You can also include information that will serve to stimulate buzz. Buzz and Wow included a McLaren brochure and a link to the McLaren website.

3. *Reminder call (two to three days before the event).* The main purpose of this call is to receive final confirmation that the client and guest will attend. This is also a good time to ask a couple of background questions about the guest.

Step 4: Conduct the Event

It's important to remember that affluent buzz is a result of your Relationship Management/Relationship Marketing Nexus. Be certain that every detail has been addressed. Often, it's the little things that stimulate buzz.

Gather background information on all attendees, and make certain someone memorializes the event by taking photos with a quality digital camera. Whenever possible, have someone take video footage with a handheld camcorder. Don't use a smart phone camera for photos or video. Buzz and Wow had the GM and one of his sales reps take photos and video.

You'll also want to prepare a quick welcome address for the group. This shouldn't be a lengthy "here's what we do for our clients" message; it should simply be, "Thanks for coming and enjoy the McLaren experience."

Once it's show time, your only task is to build rapport. Make sure everyone has a great time, and generate follow-up opportunities that fuel the buzz. Here's where your digital camera and camcorder play an important role. People love photos and video, especially of themselves. A framed photo is a nice reason to initiate follow-up contact. Uploading your video to Facebook and YouTube will generate even more buzz, making the event come to life again (this will be covered in the social media section of the chapter).

Step 5: Follow Up with Attendees

The buzz starts paying dividends *after* the event. You've already strengthened the loyalty of your affluent clients and developed a rapport with their guests. *Promptly* send each guest an email with relevant photos attached and references to the photos in your message. In addition to attaching photos in the follow-up emails, Buzz and Wow posted the video footage on YouTube and provided a link. In their email message, they suggested that the attendees show the video to their friends.

Going one step further, mail each attendee a framed photo if the event was a memorable one, such as a retirement party.

INTIMATE EVENT PLANNING FORM

Figure 4.3 is an event planning form for you to adopt and adapt.

Intimate Client Events
The Oechsli Institute Mini-Guide Series

Event Planning Form

_____
Event Title

_____
Date & Time

Venue: _____

Contact Person Name: _____

Phone: _____   Cell: _____

Email: _____

Venue Notes: _____

_____

_____

Food and Beverage Provider: _____

Contact Person Name: _____

Phone: _____   Cell: _____

Email: _____

Food Selected: _____ Quantity _____

_____ Quantity _____

_____ Quantity _____

Beverages Selected: _____ Quantity _____

_____ Quantity _____

Serving Time: _____

Food & Beverage Notes: _____

_____

_____

FIGURE 4.3   Event Planning Form

Intimate Client Events
The Oechsli Institute Mini-Guide Series

Other Event Contacts:

Name	Role	Contact Information
_____	_____	_____
_____	_____	_____
_____	_____	_____
_____	_____	_____

Cost Estimations:

Venue: _____

Food & Beverage: _____

Entertainment: _____

Departing Gift (if any): _____

Parking/Transportation: _____

Other: _____ _____

Other: _____ _____

Other: _____ _____

Other: _____ _____

Subtotal: _____

(Minus) Fund Company or Management Contribution: _____

Total Cost: _____

FIGURE 4.3 (continued)

Through our affluent sales coaching, we've witnessed firsthand how sales professionals activate and maintain affluent buzz by incorporating client events into their Relationship Management/ Relationship Marketing™ strategies. I realize that this requires a commitment of time and resources, but I've yet to encounter anyone who stopped holding these events after once trying them. (As an aside, Wow and Buzz's car events have cost them nothing: *zero* dollars.)

Intimate Client Events
The Oechsli Institute Mini-Guide Series

Client Event Checklist

Check off the boxes as you're planning the event.

☐   Select the people you would like to invite.

Clients	Potential Guests
_____	_____
_____	_____
_____	_____
_____	_____
_____	_____
_____	_____
_____	_____

COIs (if any)

_____	_____
_____	_____

Prospects (if any)

_____	_____
_____	_____

☐   Plan at least two events over the next two months. Ask guests to save the date for the second event if they cannot make the first.

Current Event: _____   Date: _____

Next Event: _____   Date: _____

FIGURE 4.3   (continued)

A bonus that accompanies intimate events is that they activate the law of reciprocity. You'll find yourself invited to social events hosted by your clients and their guests. From an affluent sales perspective, it doesn't get much better.

Intimate Client Events
The Oechsli Institute Mini-Guide Series

☐ Plan Your Invitation Script and Start Making Calls

Invitation Script: _____

_____

_____

_____

Date for invitation calls: _____

☐ Send your confirmation letter to all confirmed participants

Letter to be written by: _____

Letter to be sent on this date: _____

☐ Confirmation Calls. Make a round of follow-up calls to those who have confirmed, making sure to probe into who they are bringing as a guest.

☐ Event Preparation

Use a Google search or use www.123people.com to do some backgrounds searching on the guests of your clients. Used carefully, this can give you some talking points with these new contacts. Do not let them figure out that you've google searched them; it will seem creepy.

Plan your team's roles and responsibilities at the event:

Team Member	Event Role
_____	_____
_____	_____
_____	_____
_____	_____
_____	_____

FIGURE 4.3   (continued)

SOCIAL MEDIA

The affluent are social creatures. They like to share information, ideas, and laughs, especially with those in their spheres of influence. This is why the strategic use of social media can create a synergy from your intimate client events, your visibility campaigns, and even your surprise and delight touches. Here is where the

Intimate Client Events
The Oechsli Institute Mini-Guide Series

☐   Conduct the Actual Event. Make sure you get ample time to speak with everyone and learn as much about them as possible. Also, make it easy on yourself to see the guests of your clients at another time, without seeming salesy. You can do this by coming equipped with several tracks for follow-up already in mind (golf, lunch, another event, etc.) And don't forget to take photos of the attendees.

☐   Send out the photos you took at the event. You can do this by email or regular mail.

☐   Place a follow-up call to each client that attended and thank them for coming.

☐   Follow up with new prospects as appropriate

Prospect	Follow-Up Path	When
_____	_____	_____
_____	_____	_____
_____	_____	_____
_____	_____	_____
_____	_____	_____
_____	_____	_____
_____	_____	_____

FIGURE 4.3   (continued)

result is far greater than the sum of the parts. You create buzz through your intimate events and visibility campaign, but social media enables you to take the buzz factor to another level.

According to research by Google/Keller Fay Group, owners of smart phones, which include the majority of affluent consumers, are more likely to pass along information via the Internet. In other words, affluent consumers with smart phones are even more likely to facilitate a buzz.

Let's revisit Buzz and Wow to see how they leveraged social media to heighten and prolong the buzz. As you might recall, they memorialized their event with digital photos and video. Enlisting the assistance of the general manager and his top sales rep was a stroke of brilliance. They had video and still footage of attendees in the cars, driving the cars, and being interviewed

Intimate Client Events
The Oechsli Institute Mini-Guide Series

Client Event Debrief

Theme: _____

Date: _____

Venue: _____

Number of Attendees:

Clients: _____   Guests of Clients: _____

COIs or Prospects: _____   Your Team: _____   Total: _____

Actual Cost of Event: _____

Client Reactions: _____

_____

_____

New Business Opportunities:

Opportunity   Next Step

_____   _____

_____   _____

_____   _____

_____   _____

Other Comments: _____

_____

_____

FIGURE 4.3   (continued)

about their experiences. In effect, they were soliciting live testimonials of the McLaren driving experience from affluent car enthusiasts.

This prompted Buzz and Wow to seize the moment and get video testimonials about their financial planning services. The McLaren sales rep was skilled with the camcorder and was able to prompt all types of accolades. The general manager handled the digital camera and took photos of the entire group. Buzz and Wow then posed with each individual client and guest to produce timeless evidence of everyone having a good time.

What did Buzz and Wow do with all of this affluent buzz serum? They followed a very systematic approach outlined by Kevin, their sales coach:

- They posted all pictures on their company Facebook page.
- They tagged all attendees, the owner of the dealership, the general manager, and the videographer in each picture.
- They posted the videos on YouTube.
- They sent personal emails to every attendee, as well as the owner, the GM, and the videographer, with links to the videos.
- They checked LinkedIn to see which prospects had accounts, and then asked them to connect by sending a personalized message.
- They shot a video of themselves to the tune of "We had a great time! Thanks for coming and be on the lookout—we'll soon be posting our next event." Two weeks after this initial follow-up campaign, they posted the video on YouTube and sent another series of personal emails with links to that video.

Their affluent buzz soared off the charts. Non-car-enthusiast clients were practically begging to be invited to the next event; other luxury car dealerships were vying to host future events and, within two weeks, they obtained two new affluent clients—the owner of the dealership and one of the guests.

VISIBILITY CAMPAIGN

Everyone networks. We are naturally drawn to others who share our interests and concerns. The best affluent salespeople are highly visible in their communities. Whether you're attending social events, volunteering for a cause, raising money for a scholarship fund, sitting on the board of directors for a local hospital, participating in local politics, or dining in the right restaurants, the more visible you are in the community, the more likely you are to get clients talking about you. Why? Because you're giving people something to talk about. Not to mention, when you're out in these circles, you're able to meet new people and new prospects.

Obviously, not all visibility is good. There *are* a few dos and don'ts. Running for mayor can be a good thing, but as one big-city candidate recently discovered, revelations about a sexting hobby rarely contribute to a positive image—or healthy poll numbers. In my small southern city, one politician has been forced to declare bankruptcy in the midst of a messy divorce, all of which has been reported on the front page of the local newspaper.

Okay, so those are blatant no-nos. Here's one that's a bit less obvious.

One of our clients is a life coach who conducts most of his business by phone. One Saturday, as he entered a trendy restaurant at lunchtime, he heard somebody calling his name.

"Mark! Over here—come sit with us." It was his client and a friend of hers.

Taking a deep breath, Mark walked to the table and was introduced to the client's friend. Dressed in flip-flops, wrinkled shorts, and an old T-shirt, Mark was embarrassed to be seen by a client—and deservedly so. But he shouldn't have felt ambushed. Visibility demands professionalism at all times. While he shouldn't have to wear a blazer everywhere he goes, he should *not* dress like a hobo in public. Nonbeach shoes, pressed shorts, and polo shirt would have been fine.

GETTING INVOLVED

We find that networking opportunities fall into two categories:

1. *Social groups:* People drawn together because of the activities, enjoyment, and prestige the group affords. Country clubs are a perfect example, but there are many others.

2. *Community groups:* People drawn together because they identify with, and want to contribute to, a cause. Although we've seen one community organizer garner enough visibility and buzz to propel him to the White House, your involvement doesn't have to be political in nature. Many of these are charitable groups—an affluent hotspot.

Strategic networking leverages this natural pull toward groups. By identifying social and community groups to which your like-minded clients cluster, you'll be able to:

• Access and gain entry to these groups.
• From there, position yourself to attract attention, build friendships and trust, and use your expertise to serve their causes.

As you become a respected and a trusted member of a group, other members will seek out your services, gladly providing you with introductions and referrals within their spheres of influence. Before joining a group, however, it's important to:

1. Have an emotional attachment to the organization. Whether it's a civic-minded group or a social one, whether you're a community organizer or a member of a country club, strategic networking must center on something you're actually passionate about.
2. Have at least one affluent client (preferably more) already in the group. It's great for relationship building with that client and they introduce you to the right people.

Whenever you join an organization, get involved—become a worker bee. The impression you make in any group will be linked to your level of involvement. When you assume a leadership role, you provide more fodder for conversation—for the buzz.

SOCIAL PROSPECTING

Today's affluent are fearful of doing business with anyone they haven't gotten to know and trust. This is why social prospecting works among the affluent, and why cold calling and other less personal tactics are becoming less and less effective.

When asked "What's your biggest challenge with social prospecting?," participants in a recent survey reported that the two biggest issues were "not wanting to appear salesy" and "not having wealthy social contacts." I've seen this play out for years. Why? In many ways, the affluent can be intimidating.

For most, this is a mind game—the fear of coming across as salesy or of being rejected. I've coached many salespeople into heavy social prospecting campaigns. I would know if they were ruining their social relationships, and this is hardly the case. When I coax them into becoming more active with social prospecting, their response is usually "I should have been doing this a long time ago!"

Top salespeople consistently put themselves in positions where they meet wealthy people, develop a rapport with them, and earn the right to compete for their business.

Whenever they're in these social environments (charity functions, kids' sporting events, etc.), which is often, their antennae are activated for conversations (opportunities) to make a well-placed comment that will turn a social contact into a business prospect.

I refer to this artful marketing tactic as the "redirect." As the name implies, the redirect involves steering conversations about topical events (that are in some way related to what you do professionally) into conversations about what you're experiencing with your clients and, ultimately, what you could do for this social contact. This typically happens in three phases:

1. *Acknowledge* the prospect's comment, without getting into too much detail.
2. *Redirect* by mentioning how this affects your clients.
3. *Mini-close* by asking for an appointment.

Here are a few examples that might help:

- If you're a financial advisor and someone makes a comment to you about market volatility . . .
  1. *Acknowledge*—The markets have been rocky the past few weeks.
  2. *Redirect*—We're just working closely with our clients and making sure they're protected.
  3. *Mini-close*—We've never talked much about business, but I'd love the opportunity to sit down with you to make sure you're headed in the right direction financially.
- If you're a mortgage broker and someone makes a comment to you about rising interest rates . . .
  1. *Acknowledge*—Yeah, they have been creeping up a little lately.
  2. *Redirect*—We're still finding that most people who come into our office should refinance. Historically, we're still at pretty low levels.
  3. *Mini-close*—If you don't mind me asking, what type of loan do you have now, if any? Do you have a mortgage on your vacation property?
- If you're selling luxury automobiles and someone asks you about a new model coming out . . .
  1. *Acknowledge*—There's been a lot of buzz lately on that one. That much horsepower in that size car is impressive.
  2. *Redirect*—We've been having trouble keeping them on the lots.
  3. *Mini-close*—I've got one in now with a sport package that I've been dying to drive. You want to come by and go for a spin with me?

The pitfall for many salespeople is that, when faced with a conversation that's related to what they do professionally, they go on and on about that particular topic. They use these conversations as an opportunity to showcase their smarts. More often than not, this becomes a circular conversation, ending with the salesperson in no better position to sell than when the conversation began.

I recommend cutting these conversations short by redirecting this social contact into a more productive discussion. Essentially, you're respectfully gaining control of the conversation, getting the attention of the person who's been talking, and subtly offering your services—almost as a favor.

Here's a key point: The less you talk, the better your results. Sure, you're offering your services, but you're not explaining any details of what you do. If they ask, simply respond, "It's very involved. I'll walk you through it personally" and continue to close for the appointment.

Affluent prospects are very reluctant to work with anyone they don't yet know or trust on a personal level. This is why social prospecting is so powerful. It's 95 percent about managing relationships and 5 percent about selling. Top salespeople recognize redirect opportunities and take action.

REVISITING PAST OPPORTUNITIES

You might be thinking, "Where was this information a few months ago? I could have used it on the golf course when XYZ prospect was talking with me about XYZ topic." Have no fear: You can still revisit those situations. I recommend running the following drill:

1. *Think back.* Jog your memory over the past six weeks to when you've been out socially and faced with a conversation about something related to what you do professionally. Nearly all of these conversations, even if you didn't seize the opportunity at the time, can be revisited.
2. *Create a list.* Make note of missed opportunities from the past six weeks that includes:
   - The name of the person with whom you were speaking.
   - The topic discussed.
   - The time/place you will *reapproach* them.

3. *The right language.* It's perfectly appropriate, even weeks or months down the road, to revisit these conversations. I recommend saying something such as, "A while back, you had some questions about XYZ. I should have offered this back then, but I'd like to sit down with you to see if we can help."

This might be the quickest way to repay your investment in this book. I often find that salespeople can think of four to six examples within a few minutes.

BEWARE! TOP FIVE WAYS SALESPEOPLE APPEAR SALESY

I've seen many salespeople who weren't willing to socially prospect. They considered friends, family members, and committee members off limits. This is a "common cold" mind-set afflicting many salespeople.

In reality, most salespeople are miles away from the salesy persona they fear. It's been my experience that salespeople who are overly fearful of being salesy wouldn't come across as salesy if they tried. It's like the guy going to the gym for the first time and telling his trainer that he doesn't want to get too muscular. It's not going to happen.

Most salespeople should be more assertive when offering their services to social contacts. For that to happen, they must get over the fear of being perceived as salesy. Selling is part of the job and, besides, you probably do great work. You have to believe that, by offering your services to them, you're doing social contacts a big favor.

Let's review some of the main ways in which people come across as salesy. I think you'll find that most of these attributes are easily avoided.

1. *Talking too much.*

This usually takes the form of talking about what you do, how much you know, and how good you are. When you try too hard to make a good first impression, it usually backfires. It comes across as self-absorbed bragging, and it is salesy. From the newest rookie to the most grizzled veteran, everyone claims to be good at their craft—fully capable of serving the needs of the affluent. In social settings, talking too much about your approach, your team, and your experience is a guaranteed "prospect repellent."

2. *Sales before relationship.*

This is a relationship business. Approaching someone about doing business before letting them get to know you on a personal level reeks of "pushy salesman." An insurance agent came to our office recently to meet with one of our associates. Before he made it down the hall, he introduced himself to one of our coaches, told him all about his firm and expertise, and tried to schedule a meeting. Sales alert! Next time he sees this person coming, our coach will close his office door.

3. *Being too scripted.*

Salespeople get a fair amount of sales training—some good, a lot of it "old school." The focus on value propositions is a perfect example of antiquated salesmanship. Someone poses the "What do you do?" question at a social event, and the response is delivered as if some "play button" was just pressed. Invariably, the response is too long, too descriptive (with too much industry jargon), and comes across as disingenuous. This activates a sales alert in the prospect's mind. The affluent instantly detect and disregard scripted, salesy language.

4. *Handing out business cards.*

As innocent as this might seem, prematurely handing out business cards is old school, and in today's environment it's a turnoff. Handing out brochures is even worse. Why? Because the affluent perceive them as a sales piece, not as a helpful document that explains your services. I've also seen salespeople adopt the practice of not carrying business cards, but I don't recommend this, because it gives the wrong impression if you receive a sincere request for your card. If asked, exchange cards, but be sure to exchange cell phone numbers as well.

5. *Pushy follow-up*.

   We've all experienced overly aggressive follow-up. Some salespeople are much too obvious. You meet the person once, and he immediately tries to set up an appointment to pitch his wares. He calls too many times, sends too many emails, and has as much finesse as an M-1 Abrams tank driving through a gift shop. Follow-up is an art. Too little or too much can spell disaster.

You're *not* being salesy if you ask someone to discuss business. It's part of your role as a stand-up professional and a community steward. You owe it to yourself to offer your services when the right situation is presented.

Think of sales as shooting a basketball. If you shoot five free throws and they're all hitting the front of the rim, you'd give the next shot some extra oomph, and get the ball to the back of the rim. You're overcorrecting as a means to finding the sweet spot. The same holds true for social prospecting: If you find yourself failing to ask for the business (shooting short), you need to be a little more assertive. You might feel like you're pushing the envelope, but in reality, it's probably just the right amount of forwardness. Whether it's foul shooting or social prospecting, you've got to be *in the game* to improve your game.

Salespeople need to become skilled in the art of social prospecting in affluent circles. It's easier to develop a rapport and let people feel as though they're getting to know you without business barriers in the way—which is why the less business you discuss in social settings, the more business you're likely to obtain, if you have the right sales skills. Top salespeople understand this and have become masters of the "less is more" philosophy: less talking, more impact; less business talk, more business; less industry jargon, more sincerity, and so on.

None of this is very complicated. Affluent sales and marketing is actually a simple process for anyone who is willing to get personal and take the initiative to master the art of selling in affluent circles. Simple, yes, but easy, no.

SUMMARY

It would be impossible to cover every method for stimulating affluent buzz in this chapter. My intention was to frame your thinking around three interrelated methods: intimate events (getting social), visibility campaigns (being seen), and social media (heightening and spreading the buzz). We've seen these methods generate affluent buzz for many affluent sales professionals. But—and this is a big but—you *must* roll up your sleeves and put in the work. You must take ownership of your affluent buzz factor.

For Buzz and Wow, the results went beyond their wildest expectations. Sure, they remain first-class financial planners, but all of their marketing now revolves around the affluent buzz that has been created and spread via intimate events and social media.

Research Facts
- The typical affluent family has seven spheres of influence.
- The number one preferred event among affluent clients is one that's intimate and fun.
- The number one event to which affluent clients will bring guests is one that's intimate and fun.
- Ninety-five percent of affluent consumers cite personalized service as the major criterion in generating their repeat purchases.
- Eighty-two percent of our affluent respondents say face-to-face interaction is their preferred communication medium.
- The demographic most quickly adopting social media is those aged 55 and older.
- Fifty percent of smart phone owners say they've seen or heard something on the Internet before having a conversation with a salesperson.[1]

---

[1] Google/Keller Fay Group, Word of Mouth and the Internet Study, June 2011.

Taking Action

- Profile your affluent clients' passions; determine what they enjoy doing in their free time.
- Using the seven spheres-of-influence model, uncover connections with each affluent client.
- Schedule a fun and intimate event for five clients who share the same interests.
- Invite the selected clients by following the steps outlined in this chapter.
- Launch your social or civic visibility campaign. Get involved with a group.
- Target specific group members and look for the right opportunity to discuss business.
- Avoid the top five ways advisors appear salesy.
- Use social media to amplify and spread your buzz.
- Get the cell phone number of every affluent client.

Chapter 5   Building Personal Relationships

Developing personal relationships with the affluent significantly improves the salesperson's perceived performance among the affluent. Trust increases by 23 points, service by 22 points, communication by 19 points, and industry knowledge by 16 points.

—Factoid, 2013 APD Research

Can you imagine a world in which 44 percent of affluent buyers (36 percent of affluent women) trust salespeople, but your own ranking surpasses 90 percent because you've cultivated so many personal relationships with these prized customers? Imagine no more! The dream is not only plausible, but extremely possible. Our APD Research points to a path that follows two macro affluent shifts: gender and relationships.

A few months ago, I was in Seattle on business and, in keeping with my routine, was scheduled to have dinner with my cousin Marty. On this particular evening, we went for a seafood dinner at Chinooks, one of my cousin's favorite restaurants. As we entered, we were instantly greeted with a shout of "Hey Marty!" and a big wave from one couple. Marty waved as we were seated by the hostess and then excused himself to visit the couple.

Cousin Marty is an affluent salesman who has sold BMWs for BMW of Seattle for 20 years. Returning to our table, he explained that the friendly diners were clients who'd purchased a number of cars from him. What I also discovered was that Marty had established a personal relationship with the couple. They regularly played golf together and even went to Ireland on vacation with some other affluent golf enthusiasts.

Does my cousin vacation with all his clients? No. Does he play golf with every client? Hardly. But Marty understands the importance of forging personal relationships with each of his luxury car–buying clients. It's helped him to develop a healthy stable of repeat clients.

Whether you're selling luxury automobiles, jewelry, or financial services, broadening a customer relationship from one that's purely business to one that's also personal helps you win a higher percentage of loyal, repeat clients. The fact that your products or services also perform as promised is merely a hygiene factor—a built-in expectation.

Cultivating personal relationships is an essential component of affluent relationship management today, and also a key ingredient in *relationship marketing* within affluent circles. Marty enjoys a steady stream of referrals as a direct result of word-of-mouth influence within his loyal clients' spheres of influence.

Figures 5.1 and 5.2 provide empirical data that explain Marty's stream of referrals. Figure 5.1 illustrates that when today's affluent consumer classifies their relationship with a salesperson as "business and social," they provide nearly double the referrals of those with a purely business relationship. Figure 5.2 tells us that a business and social relationship increases the willingness to introduce by 18 percent. This is what prompted us to have a closer look at the power of affluent relationship management. As you can see, the sales professionals who were able to develop personal relationships

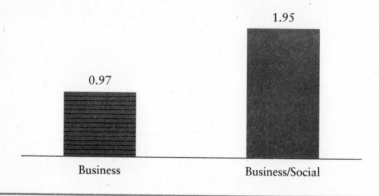

FIGURE 5.1   Referrals Given, Past 12 Months

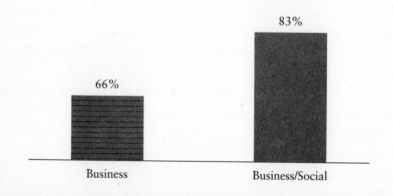

FIGURE 5.2   Willingness to Introduce

with affluent clients received nearly double the referrals and introductions as those who'd only developed business relationships.

REFERRALS VERSUS INTRODUCTIONS

Over the years, there has been plenty of misinformation about getting affluent referrals. Much of the old-style training around referrals is dead wrong. The affluent detest the typical referral request.

Asking to be introduced to someone who's connected to one of your affluent clients is the polar opposite of asking an affluent client for a referral. Yet because salespeople have been taught for so many years to ask for referrals, they tend to think of referrals and introductions as being one and the same. They are not!

Chris, a salesperson I know, recently started asking for referrals again. It had been years since he tried this tactic, and he wanted to give it another shot. The response by the first client he asked stopped this new referral program in its tracks. The client simply said, "Wow, times must be tough!"

In our workshops, whenever I ask people how their affluent clients *feel* when asked for a referral, the responses are always similar: awkward, used, uncomfortable, put upon, and so on. When asked how they feel when they ask for a referral, participants' answers are virtually the same: They don't like asking for referrals. Unfortunately, "asking for referrals" is still promoted as an effective sales tactic. Here is the truth, straight from our affluent research:

- Eighty-three percent feel uncomfortable when asked for a referral.

They're uncomfortable because this "simple" referral request puts the onus on them and prompts a multitude of other questions:

- Who do I know who is in need of this particular service?
- Who do I know who isn't happy with his or her current provider?
- Who won't be put off by me giving out their name to this pushy salesperson?

And then your affluent client replies with something along the lines of. . . .

"Let me get back to you." (In other words, "No, thanks.")

This tactic has been around a long time, but has no place in the world of the affluent. There are far more sophisticated ways of achieving the desired result (meeting new prospects through current clients). Elite salespeople orchestrate these connections in a way that *builds* the relationship between them and the client.

With personal introductions, the data works in your favor:

- Eighty-three percent will introduce you to a specific person if asked (if you have a business and social relationship).
- Sixty-six percent will introduce you to a specific individual if asked (if you have a purely business relationship).

There's a big difference in the willingness to introduce, a 17 percentage-point gap, between professionals with purely business relationships with affluent clients and professionals who've taken the time to also develop a social relationship. This is the essence of the Relationship Management/Relationship Marketing Nexus™. The more personal a salesperson becomes with an affluent client, the more natural it becomes to source names, and the more willing the affluent client is to make a personal introduction when asked.

An important point to remember is that by asking for an introduction, you are helping your client help you by identifying a specific person you'd like to meet. This is the heart of the introduction process. You're not asking "Who do you know?"—you're doing the detective work yourself (sourcing names in conversation or online) and thinking about how this introduction might take place, before even thinking about calling your client.

The standard timeline protocol is to wait a couple of weeks from the date the name was sourced (you never want to appear too eager), and then call your client to request an introduction. The wording should be direct and concise: "Bob, you mentioned that you have drinks after work with a colleague on Fridays. I'd like to meet him. Could I tag along next week?" Of course, if you don't drink, you can ask to be introduced by other means. Lunches, dinners, sporting events, and other similar functions work just as well.

In fact, I've uncovered 10 variations of this introduction approach—and there are probably 10 more. Use these to stimulate your introduction creativity:

1. *Direct:* "Matt, I'd like to meet your colleague Stephen. What would be the best way for us all to get together socially?"

2. *Two-Step Indirect:* "Matt, you mentioned that you spend a lot of time with Stephen at work. Does he know that you and I work together?" (Pause) "Great, I would love the opportunity to meet him."

3. *Recreational:* "Matt, we're looking to get a foursome together for golf this Saturday. Would you want to join us?" (Pause) "Do you think your colleague Stephen would want to play?"

4. *Social:* "Matt, why don't you invite Stephen and his wife to join us at the club's wine tasting this Friday night?"

5. *Compelling Reason:* "Matt, you mentioned Stephen's going to retire soon. You probably should introduce me to him—just to make certain he's got his bases covered. That's exactly what I do."

6. *Situational:* "Matt, are Stephen and Heidi going to be at the fundraiser this Saturday night?"

7. *Tag Along:* "Matt, next time you and Stephen go fishing, would you mind if I tagged along? I would really like to meet him."

8. *Strategic Placement:* "Matt, I'd love to attend the fundraiser—could you make certain I'm sitting next to Stephen and Heidi?"

9. *Spontaneous Situational:* "Matt, is that your colleague Stephen with his wife over there? Could you introduce me?"

10. *Online Profiling:* "Matt, I saw that you're connected to Stephen Boswell online—how well do you know him? Could you introduce me?" (follow-up statement) "Let me know if you ever want to meet any of my connections."

In reality, if you become proficient with two or three of these techniques, you'll reach elite status. The secret is arranging the personal introduction in a social venue. Why? For starters, it's more comfortable for your client to simply make the connection, not sell your services. Plus, it's easier for you to develop rapport with a prospect when business isn't on the agenda. This type of social meet-'n'-greet will require a bit of brainstorming with an affluent client about how, when, and where this personal introduction will occur. However, when your affluent client agrees to personally introduce you, they will make this quite easy.

The Great Recession fundamentally changed how the affluent view the sales and marketing of big-ticket products and services. Now it's all about word-of-mouth. Truth in advertising" is yesterday's news—if it ever *was* news at all. These days, only 45 percent of the affluent (on average) trust advertising messages. No matter what lens you use to view those statistics, it's obvious that, despite the billions of dollars spent trying to persuade affluent consumers to purchase products and services from these industries, the affluent don't believe their advertising promises.

This *mistrust factor* extends beyond advertising. From the news media to Amazon book reviews, affluent consumers no longer rely on the say-so of "experts." Instead, they've defaulted back to personal relationships as the only reliable source of trustworthy

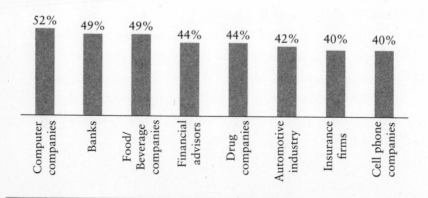

FIGURE 5.3 Trustworthiness in Advertising (Some to Full Trust)

information. They trust the recommendations of friends, family, and colleagues. They also trust the recommendations of other professionals with whom they've worked closely.

PROFESSIONAL ALLIANCES

Top salespeople understand the power of referral alliances with other professionals. With iron-clad alliances in place, they start each year fully expecting a handful of new ideal prospects to come their way—just from managing these professional relationships. This relates directly to how the affluent make major purchase decisions. We've seen Realtors work with mortgage brokers, CPAs work with financial advisors, marinas work with boat stores, and so on. Nearly every professional who is servicing the affluent has other professionals in the area who provide complementary (not competitive) services.

What other types of professionals do your clients use? Do you know the best in the area? Have you met with them? These are all questions to ask as you're building out your professional alliance strategy.

Keep in mind, it's been our experience that the best salespeople typically have four to five good partners, not 20 or 30. They manage these relationships much like they do their top clients. Frequent interaction, both social and business, is their recipe for success.

These outside professionals are invited to lunch, dinner, client events, and other social activities. They're also sent referrals when a client might need their services. This doesn't take as much time as you might think, but it does require a dedication to keeping this outside professional engaged throughout the year.

Many of you might need to find a few new alliance partners. We suggest starting through current connections. Which professionals do your clients recommend? If they're happy with a certain professional, you'd like to meet this person. If they're not happy, you could introduce them to someone else.

As soon as you identify a referral alliance partner with potential, you begin the process of getting to know them. Arrange an introductory lunch or coffee on the basis that you're both professionals in the same community or because you have a mutual client. At this point you're starting to profile them. Would they service your clients well? Do you get along with them? Do they understand how these relationships are supposed to work? Through ongoing contact you're able to filter out those professionals who aren't a good fit.

We often find that salespeople know very little about their referral alliance partners. They might know their area of expertise or the types of clients they service, but they don't know much about them on a personal level. At many of our workshops, we take people through a little exercise where they are to profile their referral alliance partners. They are to take out a sheet of paper, write down the name of a referral alliance, and begin listing everything they know about this person. This exercise doesn't take very long and you can probably guess why. How do you fare in the following challenge?

Challenge

Profile two or three of your top referral alliance partners using the following outline:

- Name:_____
- Spouse's name:_____
- Kids:_____
- Hobbies/interests:_____
- Favorite restaurants:_____
- College attended:_____
- Favorite sports teams:_____

Would uncovering the answers to these questions strengthen your relationship with this professional? Would a stronger relationship lead to more business going back and forth? You bet it would.

Managing this relationship over the long term is the biggest challenge facing salespeople with referral alliances. Many are able to initiate the first contact, but find themselves challenged to remain in contact as the days and months wear on.

There are a number of paths you can take, both social and business, to keep these partners engaged. Although the objective is to develop a business relationship, it is important to remember that it is much easier to develop rapport on a social level. Why? Because everyone's defenses are down when socializing. This is why salespeople should place more emphasis on social contacts for developing and strengthening referral alliance relationships.

This becomes easier as you get to know these professionals on a personal level. For instance, if you know any of their hobbies, sports, or recreational interests, you could organize a contact around that specific activity. If you know that a CPA and her spouse love to dine at a certain restaurant, you can suggest having dinner at this restaurant as couples.

Done properly, this strategy helps the client and the professionals involved.

GETTING PERSONAL

Getting personal doesn't always require socializing. Personalization is simply an attitude expressed through words and deeds. Do you care? Have you taken time to uncover personal information about clients and prospects? Have you engaged in extended conversations, to the extent that you truly understand customers' needs, wants, and expectations? Merely demonstrating proficiency in transactions is no longer enough. Today's affluent want a trusted professional to assist them with most, if not all, of their major financial decisions.

My clothier, Sam, is a case in point. I love Italian suits, and because I'm constantly lecturing around the world about our affluent research, these garments are my basic uniform. This often leads to compliments, which often leads to inquiries about the clothier. When I mention that he's located in Anchorage, Alaska, a look of disbelief invariably crosses the faces of my interrogators. Time permitting, I then tell them about Sam.

A salesman at Nordstrom in Anchorage, Alaska, Sam works in the men's clothing department. Although he's very knowledgeable on every aspect of men's clothing, his expertise lies in high-end business attire. My relationship with Sam began as an accidental encounter. I'd arrived in Anchorage on a Sunday afternoon to give a series of lectures the following week. Having never been to Alaska and not knowing what to expect, I left my hotel to explore. After wandering through downtown Anchorage, I decided to seek out a warmer environment, and ducked into the Nordstrom to defrost. Once inside, I wandered to the men's section to inquire about Italian suits. Mind you, I hadn't gone inside expecting to buy a suit, since I hadn't known that a Nordstrom even existed in Anchorage.

As it happened, Sam had a "very handsome Zegna pinstripe at 50 percent off" that looked as though it would fit. He explained that he'd had it delivered from Seattle for a client who'd changed his mind at the last minute. Next thing I knew, I was trying on the suit. It fit like a glove, needing only minor alterations. In the blink of an eye, Sam's tailor appeared from nowhere to take my measurements, after which he assured me that the suit would be tailored and hanging in my hotel closet by Monday the following day.

Sold! I got a good deal on a nice suit, and Sam handled the transaction in a very businesslike manner. But he wasn't finished. As we were concluding the deal, he asked if he might inquire about my profession. He wanted to know the types of groups I addressed, how often I lectured, the nature of my company, the books I'd written, the makeup of my family, how many suits I owned, how often I wore them, my preferred styles, and so on.

All of this was done in a low-key, conversational manner. I didn't feel he was prying. It was a cold Sunday afternoon and I was glad for the conversation. It wasn't until I was ready to depart that I realized I was in the presence of a *professional*'s professional—a truly polished salesman. Sam asked permission to contact me whenever he came upon a marked-down Zegna or

Canali suit or sports coat. Talk about a close! He was already asking for the next order.

I happily gave Sam my personal cell phone number and, since then, I've purchased nine suits and two sport coats. He calls two or three times a year and, though I don't always make a purchase, I often do. Only once have I had to return an item, because of a minor style issue, and I've referred Sam to my associates and to inquiring salespeople around the country.

By the way, Sam is one of Nordstrom's top salespeople—in the nation.

BECOMING SOCIAL

When people think of CPAs, the words "sales professional" are rarely top of mind, but few salespeople have mastered the relationship management/relationship marketing nexus as well as a CPA named Scott.

Ten years ago, Scott realized that, though he was an excellent CPA whose affluent clients thought highly of him, he was receiving only the occasional referral. After brainstorming with his wife, they decided to forgo a European vacation that year and invest in two big social events for affluent clients and their friends. It was a costly endeavor that pulled both of them far outside their comfort zones.

They created two themes for the events: one focused on Thanksgiving and the other on the end of tax season (April 15th). The Thanksgiving event was held two weeks before the actual holiday, and was basically a well-catered party. They had good food, plenty of adult beverages, and even door prizes. The post-tax season event took the form of a golf tournament followed by a cookout where prizes were presented.

Scott's office, which includes his wife, staged the events so well that guests were *beyond* impressed—they were delighted. The affluent clients he acquired at the Thanksgiving party more than paid for *both* affairs. Scott realized that he was onto something big. Affluent clients were continually asking when he was having his next event and talking about guests they would invite.

Scott had created a *buzz*—not because of his excellent accounting services, but through the social events. Scott got personal with his affluent clients, both husbands and wives, and his clients appreciated it. They talked about him with friends and colleagues and by the end of his second year of socializing through these events, he hired another CPA to help with the workload. He's built a remarkable practice by forcing himself to expand his relationships with affluent clients. His original strategy was to invest in high-end social events that people would talk about, but never in his wildest dreams did he think the events would become such a powerhouse marketing tool.

Our research indicates that when it comes to services, especially intangible services such as accounting, law, and financial planning/advice, performance rankings skyrocket when the practitioner broadens his or her customer relationships beyond the purely transactional. Figure 5.4 tells the story. Note the ranking

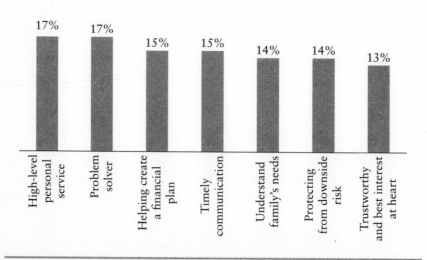

FIGURE 5.4   Financial Professional Performance Rankings: Business-Social Relationship (% Indicates Gap between Business-Only Relationship)

differences between financial advisors with only a business relationship and those who've developed a business *and* social relationships. For instance, take notice of the ranking gap in "high-level personal service"—financial advisors who had developed both a professional and social relationship scored 17 percentage points higher in providing "high-level personal service" than their colleagues who had only a business relationship with their affluent clients.

CULTIVATE PERSONAL RELATIONSHIPS

As much as frequent fliers complain about airlines (and I know this firsthand because I'm always on a plane), airlines are doing a better job of catering to the affluent than jewelers are. Thanks to improved first-class seating and more personal attention, 57 percent of affluent passengers rate airline service good to very good. By comparison, only 44 percent of the affluent gave jewelers this rating. It appears jewelers need to do more than display expensive jewelry. They need to develop personal relationships with customers.

At least airlines are *trying* to tackle the issues. They are piloting a VIP program to personalize the flying experience. According to a *Wall Street Journal* article by Scott McCartney, "The Star Treatment: Flying Like Jennifer Aniston,"[1] "Many carriers have 'special service' staffers to speed stars and VIPs through airports and on to planes, or out back doors to limousines." This program was originally designed to protect Hollywood celebrities from paparazzi, but it soon became obvious that many affluent fliers would pay more to enjoy hassle-free flying. However, as McCartney writes, "But even if you haven't won an Oscar, you can purchase a bit of special coddling for yourself for as little as $100." (American Airlines has a special "Five-Star Service"

---

[1] Scott McCartney, "The Star Treatment: Flying Like Jennifer Aniston," *Wall Street Journal*, April 1, 2008.

concierge service at LAX and New York's Kennedy International Airport.) Ironically, the same edition of my local newspaper that ran the AP article also contained a story entitled "Airline Arrival Rates Slip to 80.3 Percent." The first sentence read, "Airlines are struggling this year to get planes to the gate on time." Sorry, but no VIP Five-Star Service program will placate affluent travelers who miss their connections, especially when they've just paid a hefty surcharge for better service.

The bottom line: To successfully sell to the affluent, you must cultivate personal relationships with them. Just as important, your product or service must be *exactly* as promised—if not better. If an airline promises to fly me from Greensboro, North Carolina, to Denver, Colorado, by 5:00 P.M., and I miss my connection in Charlotte because of delays getting to the gate, I won't be a happy traveler. And I will remember this episode. And I will avoid flying with that airline again. In addition, I will tell dozens of friends, family members, and colleagues about the negative experience— in person, by phone, by text message, and via social media.

This is the mind-set of today's affluent. A product or service that delivers as advertised is supposed to be a given. Don't expect applause for doing what you promised. It's the personal touches that will transform affluent clients into long-term loyal clients. Poor products/services and a lack of personalization, however, may transform them into powerful adversaries.

THE DIGITAL IMPACT

When was the last time you researched something *big*—a serious medical problem or a major legal issue? After completing your digital due diligence, were you anxious to have a face-to-face meeting with a physician or an attorney? If so, you have some-thing in common with today's affluent. They are always seeking *personal* encounters. In fact, the more digitized affluent consumers become, the more they crave face-to-face interactions, especially when big purchases are involved.

Preferred Communication for Complex Interactions

Face-to-face	71%
Telephone	15%
Email	7%
Combination	7%
Mail	0%
Texting	0%

Preferred Communication for Simple Interactions

Telephone	35%
Email	31%
Face-to-face	21%
Combination	10%
Mail	2%
Texting	1%

These communication priorities may seem like common sense, but to paraphrase Benjamin Franklin, "I don't know why they call it common sense when so few people seem to have any." Email seems like the most time-efficient medium, but when major financial decisions are involved, email should be used only to schedule face-to-face meetings, not for completing the transactions. Even then, be sure your prospect or client uses email regularly. If not, pick up the phone and schedule a personal meeting. Do not attempt to settle the issues by phone.

When communicating with affluent clients and prospects about simple matters, a personal email is not only acceptable, it is nearly as preferred as a phone call. The key to making digital communication meaningful is keeping it personal and timely. Do not allow it to be perceived as spam.

It's important to understand each consumer's preferred method of communication. Don't try to change someone's favorite media to fit your preferences. For example, if your client lives in Miami and you're based in New York, routine face-to-face meetings are probably impractical.

Although social media is generating lots of hype, the affluent have not been as been quick to embrace it as a means of communicating with service providers (on major purchase decisions). However, a growing percentage of the over-60 crowd *do* have Facebook accounts, which they use to view photos of grandchildren and stay abreast of the grandkids' doings. Facebook is also being used by affluent sales professionals ("early adopters") to get more personal with affluent clients and prospects. Their objectives are:

1. To gather personal information about their clients and prospects.
2. To humanize themselves in front of clients and prospects by posting photos of family events, children, grandchildren, and so forth.

Although just 11 percent of today's affluent connect with most of their service providers via LinkedIn, while 35 percent connect with a "few" of their providers this way, these numbers are likely to rise as social media becomes more mainstream. For now, use face-to-face interactions to address major issues, and use the phone or email for less important matters.

Another newer communications medium worth investigating is Skype.

Honestly, I didn't know how to use Skype until our son Patrick entered a graduate program overseas and installed everything for us. However, I know early adopters who have set up Facebook and Skype accounts for clients and scored many value-added points by doing so. Again, it's important to note that these salespeople did *not* try to change their clients' preferred communications methods, but merely helped them connect with their children.

KEEP IT SIMPLE AND PERSONAL

Did Nordstrom's star salesman in Anchorage get personal? Did Sam offer me a bottle of wine, take me to lunch, or invite me to a party? Sam did none of the above. What he *did* was enhance our conversation in ways that helped him gather personal information from me—something that strengthened our rapport and built trust. Having established this base, he "earned the right" to request permission to initiate future contact if he encountered clothing I might like.

Use Sam as your guide. View every conversation as an opportunity to better know a prospect or client. Ask questions. Take your time. Be conversational. Instead of rushing to make the next phone call, meet the next potential client, or surf the Internet, prompt the prospect or client in front of you to talk about him- or herself. People love talking about themselves, their children, their careers, their hobbies, their vacation plans and so on, and the affluent are no exception.

This line of inquiry, couched in an easy-breezy conversation, is an art that's easy to learn. (For most salespeople, the hard part is developing the discipline to really *listen*.) Start the inquiry during the prepurchase phase. Uncover as much personal information as possible by linking the item being purchased to the prospect's life. Here's an example borrowed from my cousin Marty:

- What kind of driving are you planning to do with this vehicle?
- Do you have any children?
- Are they playing sports?
- Will you be carrying them around in the vehicle?
- What type of vehicle does your husband/wife drive?
- Do you participate in any recreational sports?

These sorts of questions may seem unimportant—a prelude to a lot of useless "small talk"—but nothing could be farther from the truth. They are essential to establishing rapport. Although queries must be formulated on the spot and seem spontaneous, this is easier to do than you might think. As long as your antennae are extended and ready to gather rapport-building data, your questions will come naturally.

Here's what Marty does. After supplying as much benefit/feature information as the prospect needs to make a BMW purchase decision, he asks a personal question. The question is unrelated to automobiles but it *is* related to a topic the prospect will probably want to discuss. It could be about his daughter's soccer team, the family summer home on Orcas Island—anything that will spark a conversation that allows Marty to gather more personal information.

The formula for expanding any conversation from business to personal is composed of seven parts, listed here:

1. Ask personal questions linked to the product or service you sell.

2. Use the personal information to formulate one or two personal (nonbusiness) questions, and ask them at the appropriate times.

3. Make sure you've answered every question and covered every detail of the matter at hand. Always take care of the business in a timely and professional manner.

4. When the business part of the interaction has runs its course, your goal is to extend the conversation by asking (if you were interacting with me) something like, "How is Patrick doing with his graduate program in Spain?"

5. Listen! And, if and when appropriate, ask follow-up questions.

6. The conversation should conclude with your client or prospect enjoying that warm and fuzzy feeling everyone gets after discussing their favorite subjects.

7. Enter the personal information you gathered in your system for managing client relationships, often referred to as your CRM system (or filing system).

SUMMARY

By expanding your conversations with affluent consumers from purely business to business *and* personal, your performance rankings can skyrocket in categories from perceived trustworthiness and communications ability to product/service expertise. You could easily double or even triple the number of referrals you receive from affluent clients.

The message is loud and clear: Get personal!

Research Facts

- Face-to-face communication is preferred by today's affluent for complex interactions.
- Telephone and email communication are preferred for simple interactions.
- Performance rankings by affluent clients are improved in every metric when the relationship is broadened from business to personal.
- Trust is extremely fragile with today's affluent.
- Today's affluent have a 45 percent trust factor regarding advertising in eight major industries.
- Getting personal generates nearly three times the referrals on an annual basis.

Taking Action

- Review the information you have on every affluent client, both business and personal.
- Do a little homework to gather personal information about your affluent clients by using Google or social media.
- Think in terms of spending more face-to-face time with your affluent clients and prospects.
- Look for opportunities to get social with affluent clients: civic events, community functions, sporting events, and so forth.

- Get comfortable with social media. Set up LinkedIn and Facebook accounts and connect with clients and prospects whenever possible.
- Always work to extend conversations by mastering the art (seven steps) of asking personal questions in a conversational manner and listening.

Chapter 6 Creating the Right First Impression

*Appearance, in particular how a salesperson is dressed,
is important to 67 percent of affluent consumers.*
                              —Factoid, 2013 APD Research

If you're a coffee lover, you've probably patronized both Starbucks and Dunkin Donuts during your java-drinking career. I don't mean to impugn anyone's personal preferences, but which of these two establishments consistently creates the best first impression? I've posed this question hundreds of times, and the answer is *always* Starbucks.

Not every responder likes Starbucks' basic coffee. However, the atmosphere of the cafes creates a strong (and warm) first impression. The ambience encourages patrons to stick around, spend money (not necessarily on coffee), and take a break from the day's hassles. The staff is always pleasant, pleasant music is playing, and free Wi-Fi is available. It's a simple but inviting atmosphere.

Obviously, what appears simple isn't necessarily easy, or every coffee shop in the United States would create such an impression.

None of what Starbucks does is by accident. If you want to consistently attract people who will consistently pay nearly $5 for a cup of coffee and whipped milk (latte), every detail must be carefully considered—not to mention every rule and procedure, hiring decision, training program, and inspection of what is expected. Creating the right impression requires careful consideration, planning and attention to detail. It takes work.

What mystifies me is why some of the very people who frequent these high-end cafes—people who market products and services to the affluent—haven't learned anything from these establishments. How did they miss the "first impressions" memo? Why do so many continue to make a Dunkin Donuts first impression instead of Starbucks impression?

THE GREAT RECESSION'S IMPACT

When tough times arrive, and they inevitably do, the competition for affluent dollars intensifies. Although the affluent have more resources, and are more likely to continue spending during economic downturns, they become more discriminating with their dollars. It's this kind of inclement weather that separates the well-oiled sales operation from the fair-weather storefront—the affluent sales pros from the pretenders.

Recently, a colleague was researching cleaning services for his home and his in-laws' home. After receiving three recommendations (word-of-mouth influence in affluent circles at work), he proceeded to conduct his due diligence. The first thing he did was Google each company, which led him to their three websites. He eliminated one service immediately because of the first impression created by the website: "It featured a photo of an ugly van with huge lips painted on the side and the tagline, 'Kiss Your Dirt Goodbye!' I didn't want that goofy van parked in front of my house." Otherwise, his requirements were pretty basic: The cleaning crew must speak English, be presentable (crew and vehicle), be dependable, and do a good job.

A second company failed to meet one of these criteria. The person who fielded his call spoke very poor English. The third company won the business for all the right reasons, even though the sales rep refused to quote a ballpark price over the phone. "I can't tell you until I see both homes and we determine how much work is involved." This person understood a basic tenet of affluent sales: Never quote price to an unsold prospect.

Mastering the affluent sales *process* is a requirement for any business marketing to affluent consumers. Housekeepers, landscapers, and painters are no different than luxury car dealerships, jewelry stores, home security companies, attorneys, CPAs, financial advisors, bankers, and doctors. All of them must think in terms of making good first impressions.

Many factors are important in making a good impression, including your appearance, clothes and accessories, body language, personal energy, and communication skills. A good first impression no longer depends entirely on John Molloy's "dress for success" concept. Instead, it's about dressing *appropriately* for the occasion.

This X factor was once called "class," but that aristocratic term has been replaced with "presence." Successful salespeople today have *presence*, which creates strong and lasting first impressions. In general, they also ply their crafts in environments that support their personal presence.

THE IMPACT OF ENVIRONMENT

Have you ever spent time in an Apple store? Apple has set the standard for trendy sales and service. The entire staff wears Apple T-shirts. They are equipped with iPads for Internet access and iPhones with e-readers that can quickly complete your transactions. (On my last visit, I watched an Apple staffer work patiently with a person who appeared to be both affluent and old enough to be his father.)

Yes, the sales force might have tattoos, body piercings, and unique hair styles, but their hygiene is good, their eyes are clear, and they are appropriately dressed for the occasion. The environment is pure Apple. Whether you're there to make a purchase or schedule an appointment at the Genius Bar (a stroke of genius in itself), everything screams first-class products, first-class sales staff, first-class service, first-class shopping experience!

Apple has created a buzz around their retail experience. In fact, I know professionals who have used Apple's retail facilities and staff to host intimate Apple Learning Events for their affluent clients and prospects. The salesperson hosting the event receives not only thanks from his clients, but is personally introduced to their guests. In exchange, clients and guests who attend get a hands-on tutorial for a particular Apple product.

Do you remember the last time you were in an environment (one catering to the affluent) that wasn't pleasing? Why was this? Was it poor service, a dirty facility, poorly dressed personnel, poor manners, or something else that increased the hassle factor?

I can think of many such environments—in particular, a local restaurant that hosted our holiday party two years ago. My wife and I had dined there a few times and had pleasant experiences. On this occasion, however, the service was slow, and the staff's attitude went from bad to worse when we attempted to speed up the pace. The guests were so annoyed with the experience that they vowed never to return.

Apparently, we weren't the only people annoyed with the restaurant. It went out of business 18 months later. Soon thereafter, our local newspaper ran an article that told the sad tale of how the owners had always dreamed of owning a restaurant; how they'd saved for years; and how they'd quit their jobs to launch the business. What the article failed to mention is why the restaurant failed: The couple was catering to the affluent, but didn't understand the requirements for nurturing loyal affluent clients. Their environment, while pleasant on the surface, had serious flaws. From there, negative word-of-mouth influence did its thing.

THE POWER OF PERSONAL PRESENCE

I present to sales groups around the world—usually to a company's top producers—and whenever possible, I attend the social function scheduled afterward. Each of these top producers exudes personal presence. Each is as different as an individual snowflake, but they all create a lasting impression. Forget the stereotype of the egocentric salesman, the arrogant blowhard. That caricature makes for good theater, but it's rare to find a living person who fits the description. Top professionals have good manners, dress appropriately, ask questions, listen attentively, and make you feel good in their presence.

In stark contrast are two salespeople who attended an affluent sales boot camp that my firm recently conducted. The workshop was open to the public and attracted a wide range of professionals. At lunch, I found myself seated at a table with two salespeople who dominated the conversation. At first glance, you would think they were dialed-in and eager to learn more about affluent sales.

A closer examination revealed, however, that their personal presence overshadowed everything and everyone else.

What exactly do I mean by *personal presence*? In studying elite salespeople, we've observed a certain something woven throughout their seamless sales skills. It's not quite charisma, but a combination of manners, rapport-building skills, appearance, grooming, and dress—key ingredients in defining one's personality.

The two salesmen dominating the table's conversation were textbook examples of *negative personal presence*. The one asking most of the questions was constantly interrupting whoever was talking. This is simply rude. But in addition to being rude, the man's business-casual attire (participant dress code for the retreat) was very sloppy. The other personal presence offender, though better dressed and not an interrupter, had the awful habit of talking with his mouth full. Repelled yet unable to turn away from this public display of mastication, I barely heard his questions.

Put simply, their personal presence was atrocious. No matter how eager they were to master affluent sales, their negative presence will severely damage their efforts.

In response, I tried to steer the conversation to the topic of personal presence, but the two weren't able to make the mental connection. (How do you tell someone in a public place that they have horrible table manners?) To avoid embarrassing them, I circled back to their coaches and gave *them* my feedback. I instructed them to find a proper window (a teachable moment) to hammer home these critical lessons.

EXUDING GRAVITAS (POWER POSE)

Now a popular phrase among social psychologists, *power posing* refers to personal presence—to your *gravitas*. It's a key ability when attempting to make a good first impression.

While studying research on this topic, what I found most interesting was the biochemical changes that occur when we engage in a power pose. According to research performed by Dr. Dana Carney at the University of California, Berkeley, Hass School of Business, and Associate Professor Amy Cuddy of the Harvard Business School, two minutes of a power pose elevated testosterone levels 20 percent, whereas the absence of power pose lowered it by 10 percent. That's a 30 percent variance in assertiveness.[1]

In addition to elevating testosterone levels, Carney and Cuddy discovered that two minutes of power posing lowers levels of the stress hormone cortisol. In short, it enables us to be more relaxed and confident in stressful situations.

If this is new to you, I know you probably have two questions:

1. *What is a power pose?* Basically, a power pose is good body language with a twist, since you can practice it seated or standing. Here are a few of examples:

   ○ Standing with good posture and placing your hands on your hips.

   ○ Standing with your arms raised overhead as if you just won a race. You can even pump your arms for effect.

   ○ Standing at your desk with your hands on your desk, leaning forward.

   ○ Sitting at your desk with your hands clasped behind your head.

   ○ Sitting at your desk, leaning back in your chair, with your feet on the desk and hands clasped behind your head.

   When you're interacting with your affluent client or prospect, you obviously don't want to be sitting with your feet propped on a table or standing with your hands raised over your head. Just think in terms of *open posture*—no folding of the arms or slumping when you're "in the moment." Use your common sense.

---

[1] Sue Shellenbarger, "How 'Power Poses' Can Help Your Career," *Wall Street Journal*, August 20, 2013.

2. *How do I practice?* This is something that should be done in private before a meeting, an important phone call, an affluent social event—any interaction for which you want to be relaxed, confident, and exuding gravitas. Simply execute one of the poses above, but take it a step farther: As you execute the power pose, concentrate on your breathing, making certain you are breathing through your diaphragm. Then visualize yourself in the exact moment for which you're preparing, exactly as you want to be—relaxed and confident, exuding positive energy and gravitas.

In the Harvard study, the researchers tested how people posed waiting for a job interview. Those who were high-power posers were the candidates rated as those most likely to be hired. Now we have proof that body language impacts your physiology, which can play an important role in your affluent sales success.

HOW TO MAKE A GOOD FIRST IMPRESSION

During my attempt to discuss personal presence at the lunch I mentioned earlier, I shared the following tips from Dale Carnegie's classic, *How to Win Friends and Influence People*, first published in 1937. Although the labels have changed (e.g., "class" is now "presence"), the basic concepts are timeless.

- Practice a two-minute power pose.
- Maintain a natural but strong and open posture in the moment.
- Smile.
- Show genuine interest in other people.
- Remember that a person's name is, to that person, the sweetest sound in any language.
- Be a good listener. Encourage others to talk about themselves.
- Make the other person feel important, and do it sincerely.
- Begin with praise and honest appreciation.

This is advice that everyone should follow, regardless of their profession. It should be part of your DNA.

You may have noticed that Carnegie didn't reference what we today call "dress for success." Perhaps back in 1937, when Carnegie wrote the book, people tended to dress better. Men wore suits and ties if they were dining in a restaurant, while women wore heels, dinner dresses, and gloves. Fewer people were as affluent as today, and many men owned just one or two suits, but they dressed more formally in public. As a result, Carnegie may not have felt compelled to discuss proper dress.

Unfortunately, a quick trip through an airport paints a disturbing picture of America's contemporary dress codes, or lack thereof. Sleeveless shirts, bathing suits, flip-flops, highly visible tattoos, body piercings, and poor hygiene are on display everywhere. It's unlikely that most of these people are top sales performers, but that's hardly an excuse for the sloppy, just-woke-up-with-a-massive-hangover look that so many people wear. In some instances, this is considered hip and cool—a phenomenon that has even infected the lecture and presentation circuit.

Not long ago, I was a keynote speaker at the national sales conference of a company that sells risk-management services to the affluent. It was a grand affair with all the bells and whistles. The organizers had me behind the stage as the audio people hooked up my microphone, checked the batteries, doubled checked my presentation, and so on. The speaker before me was a consultant who was talking about networking. Great topic, but as I watched him on the monitors, I tuned out his words and became absorbed in his attire. He was wearing black jeans, black rubber-soled sneaker shoes, a black T-shirt, and a black sport coat. I couldn't help thinking, "This guy's just too cool for school." Was he a Johnny Cash wannabe? Was he trying to be different? What does he wear in his office?

I discovered I wasn't alone in profiling this character. The company's senior executives, who were all wearing business attire, were thinking the same things. After my address, *The Art of Selling to*

Today's Affluent, a number of the senior managers thanked me for my emphasis on appropriate attire and expressed their disproval of the "too cool for school man in black."

Whenever you dress inappropriately, regardless of how expensive the ensemble, you get major demerits for personal presence, as well as first impression.

A HANDFUL OF SIMPLE TIPS

I've divided these tips into two categories: personal and environmental. Since the personal tips are all about you, let's start with those.

Personal Tips
- *Model the business dress of top performers.* Look at how top performers in your industry dress during face-to-face interactions with clients and prospects. This offers you a wardrobe framework within which you can work. It doesn't mean you must spend more than you can afford. I'm suggesting that you imitate the look, not duplicate it. Dress appropriately for your industry and profession. A salesperson working in a local Apple store looks good in a blue Apple T-shirt, as does the financial advisor wearing a Brooks Brothers suit in his office. These looks are polar opposites, but both are appropriate within the respective environments. Both make good first impressions.
- *Model the social (business-casual) dress of top performers.* Because today's affluent place so much importance on relationships, you'll have more social interaction with affluent clients and prospects. Therefore, it's just as important to make the right impression with your business-casual dress.
- *Model the accessories of top performers.* Women wearing too much jewelry and men adorned with pinky rings and gold chains are noticed by affluent prospects, but not in a positive

way. Whether at a social event or business meeting, you will rarely see an overaccessorized top salesperson. Top performers understand that the affluent don't respect people who try too hard to draw attention to themselves.

Speaking of attention, almost every day I encounter a salesperson who is accessorized with either tattoos, body piercings, or both. I realize that these adornments are now popular. In this day and age, you probably have a friend or family member with a tattoo or a body piercing. You might have one yourself. In affluent sales, however, the rule of thumb is simple: Make certain all tattoos and body piercings are *invisible* when interfacing with clients, in either a business or social setting. In other words, cover up.

The young lady I met the other day while purchasing a bicycle headlight was adorned in tattoos on both legs from the knee down. She was cheerful and very helpful, but the lasting impression she made was best summarized by my wife Sandy's comment: "Did you see her legs? Why would anyone want to do that?" Her appearance was fine for a retail sales clerk in a sporting goods store, but it would have been unacceptable had she been selling high-end real estate.

- *Model the grooming of top performers.* It's not just the clothes; it's how you wear them. A crisp company uniform will make a bad impression if it's accompanied by messy hair, as will clothes that are wrinkled and shoes in desperate need of a shine. When it comes to grooming, everything counts: oral hygiene, fingernails, trimmed facial hair, makeup, and fragrances. Speaking of makeup, women shouldn't use too much, and men shouldn't use any. Perfume and cologne should be used sparingly, as your scent (good or bad) should never dominate.

- *Model the personal presence of top performers.* Top performers project a positive personal presence wherever they go. Although presence may seem like an intangible quality, much of it has been learned (e.g., how to enter a room with body language that says

"I belong"). You can't go wrong by following the Dale Carnegie tips listed earlier. Displaying good manners is also part of the package. All of these ingredients constitute personal presence. Also, practice power posing to the extent that it becomes your natural pose. These are skills that were once taught in finishing schools, but they have become such a critical issue that we devote an entire segment of our Mastering the Art of Affluent Selling workshops to the topic.

As Figure 6.1 illustrates, your physical appearance (good, bad, or neutral) is critical to your branding, and personal branding is critical to sales success. Whether you're meeting clients, prospects, or centers of influence, you make not only a good first impression, but also a good *lasting* impression. This lasting impression stimulates positive word-of-mouth influence.

As you read through the following dress-for-success principles, be honest in critiquing yourself. It's easy to fall into the "that's not me" mentality. Most of us have a couple of areas that need fine tuning.

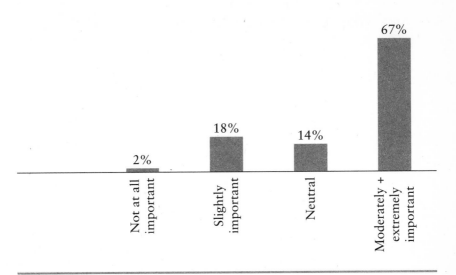

FIGURE 6.1   The Importance of Salesperson Dress

BASIC DRESS-FOR-SUCCESS PRINCIPLES

- Dress for your clients (not your friends or spouse). *It's likely that your clients and prospects, based on affluent demographics, dress conservatively. You can probably think of some examples to the contrary, but most affluent consumers dress the part. Study your target market to avoid the things they avoid—excessive hair products, hair spiking, unnatural hair coloring, box-toed shoes, popped collars, unique facial hair, and so forth. Common sense goes a long way.*
- Mirror politicians. *Model what they wear, not what they say. Most politicians wear high-quality clothing, and they wear it well. If a male politician is at a business function, he wears a suit and tie, looking as good (or better) than most of the people there. Later in the day, if he's at a pig farm, the jacket and tie are off, and the Allen Edmonds dress shoes have been replaced by a pair of galoshes. It's all about shifting gears, dressing appropriately for the occasion, but always looking spit-shined.*
- Study the art of dressing well. *There is a tremendous amount of information on this topic. Some rules are timeless; others have changed. In the late 1970s, as a young self-employed businessman earning my graduate degree at night, I read* Dress for Success *by John T. Molloy. It provided me with a clear understanding of how to make a good impression by dressing the part. The business-casual movement has made some of Molloy's advice outdated, such as no facial hair. But many of the rules still apply.*

Men's Attire

Suits—Buy good suits. The old saying "you get what you pay for" should be a law when it comes to men's suits. You will want at least two (preferably more) charcoal gray and navy blue suits. Think in terms of traditional style: two- or three-button jackets never go out of style. Avoid suit jackets with more than three buttons.

Shirts—Long-sleeved white and blue cotton dress shirts are still standard business dress. They go well with any suit, and are easily paired with a nice silk tie. Over the past few years I've purchased only no-iron cotton dress shirts, and have been very impressed. I no longer pay a dry cleaner to ruin my shirts. I throw them in the washing machine, and then in the dryer, and then on a hanger, and they're ready to wear. When they occasionally wrinkle from packing, I hang them in the bathroom while taking a shower, and the wrinkles quickly steam out. I'm also amazed at how crisp they look at the end of a day, whether I've flown across the country or delivered three lectures. A crisp dress shirt makes a very positive impression. Warning: Avoid dark dress shirts when wearing a tie. I call it the gangster-hipster look—navy dress shirt/dark tie, black shirt/white tie—you get the picture. For some reason, this look has gained traction among the uninformed. This isn't just my opinion; you never see top lawmakers or business people dressed in this attire for a reason.

Ties—Ties often reveal a man who knows how to dress. When chosen with care, the tie can be the final touch to a man's image. With such a wide selection to choose from, keep these basic principles in mind. Ties should be silk and feel supple to the touch. Stick to solids, stripes, club, polka dot, or pin dot patterns. Avoid wild patterns or cartoon characters. When in doubt, ask for help from someone who looks like he knows about ties. Be sure to tell him that the tie is for business, not a wedding.

Socks—You can have fun with your socks in business-casual situations if you're brave or, I should say, if you trust your judgment. Some men's socks have gotten quite wild. In a business setting, however, stick to the basic colors of black and dark blue. Socks are simple if you remember that they should be knee length (you don't want to reveal a hairy calf when crossing your legs) and you stick to solid dark colors.

Shoes—Good dress shoes are made entirely of leather: uppers and soles. However, some acceptable dress shoes are now made with leather uppers and synthetic soles, which are slim and made to resemble a leather sole. A lace-up shoe is the best match for a charcoal gray or navy suit, but dress loafers are also acceptable. As for colors, think black, cordovan, and brown—in that order. And make sure your shoes are shined! Again and again, I've seen first impressions take a body blow, thanks to scuffed shoes. Remember, after making eye contact while shaking hands, most people glance down. You want them to see a pair of nicely shined dress shoes.

Accessories—A good watch and a wedding ring (if you are married) are all that is required. A small computer bag is now acceptable, as is an expensive leather attaché case. You can also have a nice portfolio or a notebook. Always carry a decent pen. You will get people's attention if you're using a Mont Blanc, Waterman, or another expensive pen. However, this is an optional accessory.

Women's Attire

Suits—Conservative, well-tailored dress and pant suits comprise the classic professional look. Avoid the trendy, and stick to solid colors like black, navy blue, and beige. These outfits will always be in style.

Blouses—Conservative is the rule. Cotton or slick shirts that reveal very little (if any) cleavage are best. Be sure to coordinate your colors and patterns with your suit.

Shoes—Think normal "pump" dress shoes, with a low to moderate heel that matches the suit. These will provide the professional business look you want for affluent sales. Be careful with heels: too flat (unless you're extremely tall) might come across as too casual, while spiked heels might not give the right impression to affluent clients—male or female.

Hosiery—In a professional setting, the rule of thumb is that the shade of your hose should be similar to the color of your skin. Avoid hosiery that is patterned or has decorations of any type. Support hose are acceptable if you're going to be on your feet all day or you're flying long distances.

Accessories/Jewelry—When it comes to jewelry, think understated elegance. A nice watch, a wedding band (if you are married), quality earrings, an elegant bracelet, and a clean necklace are always in fashion. Be sure to keep everything basic in size. You don't want jewelry to be oversized or obnoxious. Your jewelry should complement your appearance, not define it.

Purses should be small to medium sized; leave the oversized purse in the trunk of your car. Your attaché or computer bag should also be a small to medium size. The rule of thumb is that a purse or attaché/computer bag should be in good proportion to your height.

Be careful with perfume. You don't want your scent entering the room before you arrive, or lingering after you leave. Also, keep in mind that some people have allergies. You don't want a client sneezing throughout your presentation.

You want to be perceived as successful, professional, and trustworthy—personal traits that are enhanced by dressing properly for the occasion. Every affluent sales person should think of him- or herself as an extension of the product and the brand. If you're in the intangible world of services, *you* are the product. You represent the brand. The hard reality is this: If the affluent perceive you as a little too sloppy, a little too cool, a little too young, a little too old, a little too [anything they don't like], you decrease the odds of conducting successful transactions with them. Therefore, it literally pays to ensure that your wardrobe is up to snuff. Fortunately, this is one of the easiest and least expensive ways to enhance your professional brand.

Making a good first impression goes beyond the aforementioned. We all know someone who, despite buying quality garments, seem to always look disheveled. In your quest to consistently make a good impression, the following list might serve as a helpful reminder.

- Wear clothing well. *There's nothing worse than a quality suit that's worn poorly. The secret is to wear your professional clothes as though you love them. Make certain your shirt is tucked in, your pants are pulled up (affluent consumers are not impressed with low-riding pants), and that you're wearing a good quality belt. Avoid slouching, fidgeting with your jewelry, or playing with your pockets. Men: If you're wearing a tie, make sure you wear it with the pride of a top performer. Too many men wear ties as if they hate them. People who seem "comfortable in their own skin" appear more confident and successful, which is exactly the image you want to project. And remember, keep those shoes shined!*

- Stay self-aware. *Dressing appropriately to your circumstances is a fluid, ongoing process. Many people (especially men) take a one-time initiative to upgrade their wardrobes, and then neglect the issue for months or years. Setting a budget and monitoring your spending enables you to combat two wardrobe problems—spending too little or too much.*
- Your out-of-office wardrobe counts. *Going grocery shopping in your flip-flops and workout shorts, without taking a shower, means you will bump into an affluent client or prospect. Odds are high that you don't want the person to see you like this, so make an effort to prevent it. Because affluent sales has become a 24/7 affair, what you wear outside your work environment counts. It also represents your personal brand. Social prospecting is the core of relationship marketing, so whether you're in a grocery store or at the beach, dress smart.*
- Shop smart. *Dressing well doesn't have to kill your budget. Buying brand-name clothing at off-season discounts is an excellent way to find quality clothing that will give you a terrific look without breaking the bank. You can also follow my routine. I look for end-of-season sales, and consistently find quality items marked down from 50 to 75 percent. Sam, my clothier in Anchorage, only calls me about a suit if it's a brand and style that I wear and it's marked down by 50 percent. I even know people who have had success using eBay. You may be gambling with suits, but you can safely hunt for ties, purses, and other accessories. It also helps to ask around. If you know someone who has mastered the concept of dressing for success, offer a sincere compliment and ask for recommendations. Well-dressed people are great resources.*

These are simple principles for dressing in a way that helps, not hurts, your chances of making the right impression. Are there exceptions to these rules? Sure. *You* must be the judge of what works in your market. However, in the world of affluent sales, where relationship management is directly linked to relationship marketing, your personal brand can make or break a deal.

To build a better business environment for your prospects and clients, use the following checklist as a guide:

Environment Checklist
- Warm and inviting
- Product or service appropriate
- Easy to navigate and clean
- Client centric (hassle free): quick, time-efficient, problems solved, questions answered, and so on
- Please come back (Apple, Starbucks, etc.)
- Parking (easy, free, and accessible)
- Safety (parking, neighborhood, in your facility)
- Cars (employee cars need to be clean and presentable, but out of the way)

SUMMARY

The affluent consumer has spoken: Dress for success is back (if it ever really went away). Over two-thirds of today's affluent have reported that how a salesperson dresses, as well as his or her overall appearance, is very important in their decision-making process. This is not to suggest that you must look like George Clooney or Cameron Diaz. Yes, I know about the research that says people are drawn to those who are considered physically attractive. However, if physical beauty were a criterion for mastering affluent sales, a number of top performers would not qualify.

Research Facts
- A salesperson's appearance is important, according to 67 percent of affluent consumers.
- Your environment (office, store, online presence) has a direct impact on first impressions.

- Eighty-nine percent of affluent consumers rate "personal inspection or consultation" as number one in importance when conducting their initial search.
- The preferred medium of communication for complex interactions (major purchase decisions) is face-to-face, according to 71 percent of affluent consumers.
- Two minutes of power posing elevates testosterone levels 20 percent while lowering levels of the stress hormone cortisol.
- Thirty-five percent of today's affluent consumers use LinkedIn to connect with service providers—and that figure is growing daily.

Taking Action
- Assess your personal appearance and compare it with top performers in your industry.
- Make necessary adjustments to ensure that your appearance models the top performers.
- Assess your environment (office, store, online presence) to make sure it's professional, warm and inviting, and encourages major purchase decisions.
- Practice your power poses.
- Ask a family member or friend to read this chapter and give you objective feedback on the first impression that you and your business environment make.

v

Chapter 7 Today's Affluent Female

Today's affluent women are far more educated than nonaffluent women: 44 percent of affluent females completed graduate school, compared with 7 percent of nonaffluent females.

—Factoid, 2013 APD Research

Since the Great Recession, subtle and not-so-subtle changes have affected how the affluent make major purchase decisions, and no change is more important than the growing influence of the female head of the household.

Remember the Elliots—the couple who bought the luxury beach home? A few years ago, Mr. Elliot was on a business trip when he happened upon a wholesale jewelry store that sold to the public. Once inside, he was magnetically drawn to a woman's 18-karat-gold watch and its discounted price. After a brief internal debate, he bought the watch for his wife and had it shipped to his house to avoid the sales tax. (At $10,000, the tax would have been significant.)

Because he used a credit card to purchase this luxury item, however, Mr. Elliot unwittingly prompted his ever-vigilant credit card company to issue a potential-fraud alert—a warning that took the form of a call to his home, where Ms. Elliot answered the phone. She had no idea that her husband was planning to surprise her, and noted that the credit card wasn't one Mr. Elliot normally used for business. She agreed with the customer service rep, therefore, that it would be prudent to suspend the card.

Ms. Elliot wondered what in the world her husband was doing. "Either he lost the card and doesn't know it," she thought, "or he's buying things he shouldn't. I'll wait until he calls me in a panic when his card is declined."

As luck would have it, Mr. Elliot didn't use the card again during the trip. By the time he returned, the package containing the watch was resting on the kitchen table, unopened.

Later, while placing the watch on her wrist, Mr. Elliot was shocked and crestfallen by his wife's response to the gift. "I can't believe you spent nearly $10,000 on a watch. The bank called to verify it was you. Why didn't you check with me before spending that kind of money?"

End of discussion. His next (and only) move was to contact the jeweler to arrange the watch's return.

TEACHABLE MOMENTS

At first glance, you wouldn't think the jeweler could have done anything to salvage the sale. On closer inspection, however, two teachable moments come into focus:

Teachable Moment 1: The jeweler could have engaged Mr. Elliot in more conversation about the purchase. Who was receiving the gift? Was it a special occasion—a birthday, anniversary? What kind of jewelry did his wife wear? What kind of watches did she own? What were her favorite brands? By soliciting more information, he might have steered Mr. Elliot toward a watch that would have been too good for Ms. Elliot to resist.

Teachable Moment 2: The jeweler could have asked to speak with Ms. Elliot to develop a rapport with the female head of the house. By establishing a level of trust with Ms. Elliot, the jeweler would have increased the chances that she might contact him in the future to discuss her jewelry preferences and/or to purchase something.

Granted, this jeweler's main business was wholesale. He didn't have much experience with affluent retail clients (other than online contact). Still, it's likely that *most* retail jewelers would have fallen into the same trap: completing a major transaction without asking questions about the lucky recipient and, if the item was returned, failing to reach out to the would-be recipient to build a relationship. This situation is another indicator of the impact that affluent females have on major purchase decisions.

To sell products and services to the affluent, it's essential to understand affluent women. They are different from their male counterparts. The following table illustrates a not-so-subtle gap between men's and women's trust of advertising.

Trustworthiness of Advertising (Some to Full)

Affluent female	38%
Affluent male	49%

When it comes to trust in advertising you would think that a basic requirement of every narrative would be at the very least *some*, with the objective of *full* trustworthiness. Neither gender scored north of 50 percent of this level of trust, but the affluent female proved much more skeptical. This finding should cause the billion-dollar-plus advertising industry to sit up and take notice. While the highest ranked industries and professions scored no higher than 44 percent with affluent females, four industries scored below the abysmal average of 38 percent. I'm not listing the following to single them out (there's not much difference between 38 percent and 36 percent), but rather to highlight the seriousness of this issue.

Affluent Trustworthiness in Advertising

Automotive	36%
Financial advisors	36%
Cell phone companies	35%
Insurance companies	33%

Depending on your perspective, the proverbial glass is either half empty (affluent women place little trust in advertising messages) or it's half full (there are tremendous opportunities available to increase affluent sales by building trust with affluent females, since so few salespeople are capitalizing on the gender shift).

I'm an optimist at heart. I believe that taking affluent females seriously will, in and of itself, set you apart from your competition. Layer onto that the affluent sales skills you've acquired and you'll find yourself assuming a leadership role in your company and your industry.

To better understand affluent female skepticism, let's examine female versus male attitudes toward financial advisors. It's important to note that, before the Great Recession, the male head of the household typically managed the interactions with the financial advisor. This has changed dramatically, so keep your eye on the plus symbols. These indicate the percentage of women (over men) who believe that a particular sales/service criterion is important.

- Breadth and depth of industry knowledge   +12%
- Listening and understanding my family's needs   +12%
- Providing personal and timely, not mechanical,
  communication   +20%
- Protecting investment from downside risk   +16%
- Delivering high-level personal service   +14%
- Helping create a financial plan and keeping it current   +22%

In the male-dominated world of finance, today's affluent females are telling advisors that they demand to be taken seriously. Whether it's the technical depth and breadth of knowledge, or the softer understanding of a family's needs, affluent women rank all of these criteria more highly than affluent men. What these differences tell us is that financial advisors who invest the time and energy in developing relationships with affluent females will have a distinct advantage over competitors who don't.

As a lover of sports, I'll use free throw percentages (the shot a player takes from the foul line after being fouled) as an analogous metric.

If one player shoots 80 percent from the foul line, but a teammate shoots 60 percent, the opposing team will do everything possible to avoid fouling the first player. They'd rather send the second player to the foul line. A 20 percent differential is a large gap in the game of basketball.

In the affluent sales game, a 12 percent differential is a large gap. In some respect, both genders are in sync. For example, just two percentage points separate the sexes when it comes to how important a warranty is to the final purchase decision (78 percent for males versus 80 percent for females). On the other hand, eight points separate the sexes when it comes to the ease of returning/obtaining a refund (74 percent male versus 82 percent female). While this is hardly earth-shattering news, every affluent salesperson should be aware of the attitudinal differences between affluent men and women. Every salesperson should know that winning the trust of the female head of the household is a vital ingredient in today's affluent sales recipe.

PARADISE LOST

Sally and Linda were college roommates who remained close over the years. Educated and affluent, and with birthdays falling just two weeks apart, they decided to embark on a luxury cruise for their sixtieth birthdays. After doing their homework, they booked their adventure, which included onshore activities such as swimming with the dolphins, kayaking, and photography tours.

How was their experience?

In Linda's words, "It was quite the adventure." *Translation:* Not so good.

"You'd think they'd give you a welcome packet as you board the boat," Linda said. "There were 12 floors, we didn't have a map, and it took forever to find our room."

Sally added, "You'd think they'd have a daily schedule posted by the elevators, so we'd know the events of the day. They always had so much going on, but we had to go back to our room and turn on the television to see the day's listings."

These annoyances were minor compared with what happened during onshore excursions. Although the activities were booked in advance, the women soon discovered that hidden fees were due. Then, they got separated—with Linda swimming with dolphins and Sally going kayaking. The dolphin swim went well, but Sally's kayaking experience left her livid.

"We were only in the kayak for 30 minutes, but they made us purchase a locker for that time. After the kayaking, as we were about to walk to some waterfalls to take photos, they pushed us to buy another locker for our cameras. How in the world are you supposed to take pictures if your camera is in some stupid locker? I said, 'No, I'm taking my camera and I'm not going into the waterfall.' Next thing I know, I've reached the top of the falls and I'm surrounded by vendors—peddlers. They were everywhere. I didn't feel safe. I was stranded among hundreds of aggressive Jamaicans street vendors. I had to pay someone to direct me back to the boat, which was a 15-minute walk away. I'll never go to Jamaica again, and I doubt if I'll ever take another cruise."

This is a perfect example of why the affluent don't trust advertising. This cruise line promised a few days in paradise, but it delivered unexpected fees, salesmen disguised as tour guides, and pushy peddlers. Sally and Linda booked the luxury cruise to enjoy a taste of the "good life." They expected to be pampered for their birthdays. Instead, the cruise became a voyage of the damned—a forced march through gauntlets of scheming salespeople who were eager to deliver minimal service for a maximum price. Between the hotel and airfare, Linda and Sally paid over $3,000 apiece to subject themselves to these hassles.

Need I even remind you that affluent vacationers pay good money for the express purpose of *escaping* from the petty annoyances of their everyday lives? The last thing they want is more irritation and frustrations on a carefree getaway.

What can a salesperson do to overcome this distrustful mindset? With the cruise line as an example, let's examine some steps that should have been taken:

Step 1: Whoever booked the cruise should have been responsible for *clearly* explaining every detail. There should have been no surprises—no hidden costs and no activities outside the company's control. This is a basic rule for dealing with the affluent: Be clear and honest, know the strengths and weaknesses of your products and services, and make sure the customers understand *exactly* what they're paying for so you can manage their expectations.

Step 2: Though this trip was booked by phone (no face-to-face interaction), the cruise line representative should have taken time to develop a personal relationship with Sally and Linda. Yes, this can be done over the phone. All that's required is taking the time to ask a handful of questions: When was the last time you took a cruise? Are any other family members joining you? Are you celebrating a major milestone in your life? And so on. The answers should have been entered into a passenger database. Then, Sally and Linda should have been connected with a personal "relationship manager"—the equivalent of an account executive charged with managing their experience. Before the booking was complete, the representative should have offered his name and direct phone number so they could call with any questions or concerns.

Step 3: Sally and Linda should have been met in the passenger boarding area by the relationship manager, who would give each a folder containing everything they needed to know for the next seven days, including a detailed map of the ship, a daily schedule of events, special activities, onshore excursions, and a method of contacting the relationship manager if they had any questions (or in Sally's case, if she got lost during an excursion).

Step 4: The relationship manager should have contacted the pair every other day (at a minimum) to touch base and ensure they were having a good time. With approximately 2,500 passengers and more than 1,000 crew members on the ship, delivering this level of personalized service wouldn't have been unreasonable. Even if 500 of the crew were mechanics, chefs, and janitors, this leaves 500 crew members to attend to the personal needs of 2,500 guests—or one relationship manager for every five guests.

Step 5: Onshore excursions (and other activities off the ship) should have been thoroughly vetted and carefully supervised by crew members. Every additional expense, including locker fees, tips, entry fees, and so forth, should have been mentioned in advance.

Step 6: Guests should have been "surprised and delighted" on their last day. The relationship manager could have taken photos of Sally and Linda throughout the week, given them a high-quality sun visor (featuring the cruise line's logo on the front and contact information on the back), or even a gift certificate for use when booking another cruise. These unexpected extras can go a long way toward building goodwill, trust, and long-term relationships which, in turn, can create loyal, repeat customers.

Step 7: The relationship manager should have made follow-up contact—a phone call, note, or an email—to ensure Linda and Sally got home safely, and to express the company's appreciation for their patronage.

Why is all of this so important? Read on. . . .

THE AFFLUENT FEMALE'S "GIFT OF GAB"

Although word-of-mouth influence is a major factor in how the affluent make major purchase decisions, recent studies tell us that women place more emphasis on word-of-mouth information than men. We've also learned that women engage in more word-of-mouth and are more convincing than their male counterparts when it comes to recommendations.

As reported in *Forbes*,[1] this has "huge implications for how marketing strategies need to be set in today's social age." The article reports several facts from research conducted by the Keller Fay Group, including:

- Women talk about 13 percent more brands each week than men.
- Women are more strongly impacted by word-of-mouth.
- Women's opinions and recommendations are more influential than men's by 58 percent to 50 percent.

These findings reinforce our 2013 APD Research regarding the role that affluent women play in major purchase decisions. Not only are women major influencers within their households, they are major influencers in their respective spheres of influence.

---

[1] Ed Keller, "The Gift of Gab: Women and Word of Mouth Advocacy," *Forbes*, August 10, 2012.

TOP TURNOFFS

Now that we know affluent females are more likely to talk about you and your services, here's where it gets personal: Unless you own the company, you can't control your firm's advertising messages. As a salesperson, however, you *can* control how you interact with affluent prospects. To start, please note the gap between affluent male's and affluent female's top turnoffs toward salespeople:

Affluent Female	Affluent Male
1. Too pushy—44%	1. Too pushy—30%
2. Lack of knowledge—22%	2. Lack of knowledge—18%
3. Talks too much—9%	3. Talks too much—11%

The affluent female is far more sensitive to pushy salespeople than males, although this complaint also ranks at the top of male turnoffs. Being viewed as pushy is the result of a number of factors, but it usually starts with not listening, followed by too much enthusiasm devoted to features and benefits explanations, followed by asking for the order too quickly. For affluent women, being too aggressive about your product or yourself is a huge turnoff.

Although neither males nor females like salespeople who overwhelm them with stereotypical features-and-benefits pitches, their second biggest turnoff is lack of knowledge. The affluent female wants you to make it easy for her to ask questions, so your knowledge must go beyond just the product or service. You need to know how she feels about your product or service. You need to discover what has prompted this major purchase search. And when you ask these questions, you must proactively listen. Too many salespeople know the products but not their affluent prospects. Others know their own products, but not the competition's products. Today's affluent female wants you to be a consultant.

Forget sales for a moment; nobody appreciates someone who talks too much—someone who doesn't listen or who talks incessantly about him- or herself. Period!—much less an aggressive salesperson who talks too much in an ill-fated attempt to make a sale. The best salespeople have learned to shut up, ask questions, and then listen. Today's affluent female wants to be heard. She wants to be understood.

Although both genders named these factors as their top three turnoffs, a 14-point spread separates men and women on the number one turnoff: salespeople who are too pushy. Justified or not, affluent women tend to think salespeople are pressuring them. This too-pushy perception is their all-too-real reality. This tells us that the root of the affluent sales problem goes deeper than the pitches. The problem lies with poor relationship marketing.

Sales professionals must be very patient and answer *all* the questions posed by affluent females. This requires active listening. It also requires answering seemingly naïve questions, which affluent women aren't embarrassed to ask. The male might not ask "How does that really work?," but the female will. You must ensure that your prospect or client understands the answers.

Salespeople *must* take the time to develop a rapport with their affluent female prospects before moving to close the deals. They must focus on earning trust. To succeed with affluent women, salespeople must come across as trusted consultants rather than eager salespeople.

FIVE STEPS TO STRENGTHEN YOUR RELATIONSHIPS WITH AFFLUENT WOMEN

Step 1: Take a detailed inventory of your male affluent client base, taking special note of:

- Each person's marital status.
- If married, the current status of your relationship with the female of the household.
- The last time you had a personal communication with the female of the household.

o Your knowledge about the female's likes, dislikes, her family, and so forth.

o Communication style preferences: Do you talk with her about facts and figures or how she feels about the product or service? Emotions play a large role in both genders when making major purchase decisions, but the affluent female pays much more attention to how she *feels* about something.

Step 2: Phone the female of the household to:

o Inquire about the status of the product or professional services purchased.

o Work to initiate a natural dialogue that touches emotional cords, making it safe for questions to be asked.

o Develop personal rapport. Inquire about children, vacation plans, and so forth.

o Provide your personal cell phone number, with assurances of 24/7 access.

Step 3: Follow up the call with a personal note. Because handwritten notes are a rarity these days, they stand out in the sea of junk mail. Your objective is to:

o Continue to build trust.

o Distinguish yourself from the competition.

o Thank her for her business.

o Increase the likelihood of repeat business and positive word-of-mouth within her affluent circles.

In short, go the extra yard. None of this is complex, but few salespeople invest the energy to go that extra yard, especially with the women of affluent households.

FEMALE TO FEMALE

At a workshop last year, one of the saleswomen in attendance (Laura) pulled me aside during a break and whispered, "I've got a problem. I don't think the wives of my affluent clients like me." Before you rush to any assumptions, this woman was a well-kept professional who was in her mid-fifties. And it wasn't that she was any kind of threat to these wives. However, something else was missing in the relationships she was trying to develop with these affluent clients.

After discussing the matter further, she had an epiphany: "I just figured it out. I've always focused my attention on the man of the household, simply *assuming* I'd be able to connect with the woman." In short, Laura wasn't treating the women as clients.

Female salespeople are usually better at establishing relationships than men. Women tend to be more nurturing and empathetic. That being said, it's important for saleswomen to use these relationship skills with the female of the household. Develop a healthy relationship with an affluent female and the male will follow.

CONNECTING

In an article titled "What Do Women Want? Just Ask," Niki Leondakis, chief operating officer of Kimpton Hotels, said, "Women are making 70 percent of travel decisions, for the family, for their own getaways, or for people at work. It's surprising that more people are not including women in their marketing." The same article cites the case of a leading Canadian home builder in Calgary, Alberta. In an area booming because of oil and gas, Shane Homes was building cookie-cutter homes as fast as they could process the orders. However, after the head of sales and marketing, Shane Wenzel, heard a speech at a real estate conference on the purchasing power of women, he changed his company's entire approach. "He set up small 'listening groups' of women to tap into the needs of people who actually lived in the company's homes. What Mr. Wenzel heard wasn't pretty. 'The ladies didn't hold back once,' he said. 'They were brutally honest.'

"The kitchens in the company's homes, the women said, were all wrong. The pantries were tiny, and the sinks needed to overlook a window so the kids in the backyard could be monitored. And the mudrooms! They shared space with laundry rooms, meaning that dirty floors might sit right beneath clean laundry."[2]

Connecting with the female of the household is no more complicated than what's implied in the title of the article: Find out what she wants. Find out what's important to her as it relates to your product or service. And this should go without saying: Listen patiently, probe with additional questions, and then take appropriate actions.

Connecting with the affluent women in your market will build your reputation and strengthen your personal brand faster than anything else. Even if they don't have an immediate need for your wares, they may have a friend who needs that product or service.

SUMMARY

The affluent gender shift is real and will only become more pronounced. Today's affluent female cannot be taken for granted. She is far more educated than her nonaffluent counterpart and has little trust in advertising messages.

If you're able to connect with her, you will become the beneficiary of positive word-of-mouth influence. Remember, the opinions and recommendations of affluent women are deemed more credible than those of affluent men.

Don't approach the gender shift with trepidation. This represents an opportunity to grow, since the earnings of affluent women are projected to steadily increase. Some projections claim they will outpace those of men. What we know for certain is that most women will outlive men, and in today's world, the affluent woman is a key player in every major purchase decision.

---

[2] Mickey Meece, "What Do Women Want? Just Ask," *New York Times*, October 29, 2006.

Research Facts
- Only 38 percent of affluent women consider advertising claims "trustworthy," versus 49 percent of affluent men.
- With regard to salespeople, affluent women said:
  - Forty-four percent of women think salespeople are "too pushy," versus 30 percent of men.
  - Twenty-two percent of women said salespeople "lack knowledge," whereas 18 percent of men said this.
  - Eleven percent of affluent men said salespeople "talk too much," while just 9 percent of affluent women cited this problem.

Taking Action
- Take inventory of your affluent clients and determine who you have a relationship with, male or female.
- Contact two female affluent clients a day as a "follow-up" to their family's purchase with the objective to develop rapport.
- Uncover one bit of personal information from each of your female affluent client daily contacts.
- Keep current records of your female affluent client contacts and information gathered.
- Take one personal action a day to strengthen your relationship with your female affluent clients using the information you've gathered.

Chapter 8 The Emerging Affluent

Twenty percent of American households with at least $100,000 in annual income are Millennials (aged 18 to 30) and 33 percent belong to Generation X (aged 31 to 47).

—Factoid, Ipsos MediaCT's 2012
Mendelsohn Affluent Survey

During a family weekend at the beach, I went shopping for dinner with my sons-in-law. When we reached the beer aisle, we were pleasantly overwhelmed with choices. Knowing which craft beer to choose has become as much an art as selecting a good wine. As someone who enjoys both beverages, but who's never invested enough time to become an expert, I rely on the recommendations of others. Good old word-of-mouth influence.

Before I could put on my glasses to read the labels, one of my sons-in-law put his iPhone to good use. Logging onto the Beer Advocate app, he began ticking off the names of highly ranked beers. Within five minutes, we made our selections—all of them new to me.

I was impressed. Neither son-in-law can be classified as affluent—yet. Both are professional, well-educated, high-income earners with serious potential. They are diligent in researching their purchases, and they *do* spend money. In this instance, neither gave a second thought to paying a higher price for what they considered top-quality products.

THE GENERATIONAL DIVIDE

In most sales training, prospects are treated as a homogenous group. This is a mistake. Our research is clear about the gender differences among the affluent. Now it's time to examine generational differences. As the following table illustrates, 55 percent of households earning $100,000 or more are Millennials or Generation Xers.

American Affluents Generational Age Breakdown *(September 2012)*	
Millennials (18–30)	20%
Generation X (31–47)	33%
Boomers (48–66)	39%
Seniors (67+)	8%

The basic school of sales training approaches affluent consumers as a high-dollar niche to be treated with kid gloves. The
focus is predominately on product knowledge—the type that
requires recitation of the proverbial features and benefits. That's
about as granular as affluent sales and marketing gets. This
"group think" approach assumes that as long as salespeople
explain features and benefits, they'll make the sale. That type of
thinking, my dear reader, is yesterday's news. Today, an affluent
salesperson, at the very least, must be aware of age, gender, and
personality.

Nothing highlights generational differences more clearly than
technology. Spend time with anyone under 40 and you're likely
to witness your version of my craft-beer-meets-digital-era experience. The emerging affluent were born and raised in the digital era.
They scan items in retail stores with bar code apps, read books on
their Kindles and iPads, and do a tremendous amount of digital
research before (and during) shopping.

These generational differences must be appreciated and understood by anyone attempting to market products and services to
this demographic. That being said, there are also many similarities
between the generations that shouldn't be overlooked.

The importance of digital technology to the affluent is never
far from the surface. Take the luxury automobile market. Every
luxury car manufacturer, from BMW and Mercedes to Lexus and
Volvo, has invested heavily in attracting the emerging affluent to
their brands. They've created smaller, less expensive models, and
trained a significant amount of marketing on this group. Why?
Because the automobile industry isn't as stupid as it's sometimes portrayed. Automakers know that if they can induce a first
purchase of their luxury brand, they will dramatically increase the
probability of a second purchase. The goal is to capture the emerging affluent for their brands, for a lifetime.

The emerging affluent comprise people who will diligently
research models, options, and prices in a calculated effort to obtain
the best value from every dealership within a 100-mile radius. All
this will be done on their smart phones while drinking a latte

at their favorite Starbucks. It behooves the automotive industry, if they are serious about wooing the emerging affluent, to promote consistency among their dealerships—consistency in pricing, options, environments, the service departments, and the quality of salespeople. Until this occurs, the younger generations will pit one dealership against another. They will *buy* the vehicle, but will be less likely to generate positive word-of-mouth influence about the experience.

WORD-OF-MOUTH POWER THROUGH SOCIAL MEDIA

> Fifty percent of Millennials check their email and Facebook pages within 30 minutes of waking up.
> —*Stephen Kraus, Chief Research and Insights Officer, Ipsos Mendelsohn*

Not only do Millennials conduct a tremendous amount of digital prepurchase research, they recognize the power they possess as consumers, thanks to social media. A recent "guy trip" to Key West offers a textbook example. Five Milennials in their early thirties were taking a three-day vacation to Key West. They met nearly a decade earlier while in graduate school getting their MBAs. All had good jobs, and all fit the profile of the emerging affluent. But their trip hit a snag from the get-go: The connecting flight was canceled and the airline provided no help—no alternative flights or hotel accommodations. Nothing.

MBA Grad 1 takes out his cell phone, calls the airline, and pleads his case in the standard manner. He gets nowhere and, to add fuel to the fire, he finds himself being mocked by his friends. MBA Grad 2 pronounces, "Let me show you how to get results." He calls the airline, explains the dilemma in similar terms as the first caller, gets stonewalled in a similar fashion, but then adds, "This is ridiculous! I've got over 2,000 Twitter followers and I'm going share this experience in detail. I bet it will go viral."

The airline's tone changes immediately. They provided the group with hotel accommodations for the night, complete with dinner and breakfast vouchers, as well as personal ground transportation to and from the hotel. Thank you, social media!

Please don't get the impression that social media rules the day, because it doesn't. What digital social networks provide is transparency regarding customer experiences, especially Millennial and Generation X experiences.

This past Mother's Day created a near-death experience for a major online florist. Apparently, a number of orders were messed up—to the extent that the company received an avalanche of scathing complaints. The complaints were posted individually on each client's Facebook page. The negative messaging went viral.

Fortunately, this florist was proactive and resourceful. In a matter of days, they turned the negative word-of-mouth campaign into a positive story by sending new bouquets to each aggrieved customer—each larger than the original order and containing a note of apology. Within minutes of the unexpected surprise, Facebook posters did an about-face, posting comments like: "This is so thoughtful" and "I can't believe [florist] sent a larger bouquet than originally ordered with a note of apology. I'm now a customer for life." Once again, the news went viral, replacing the negative rants and enabling the company to make a lasting and *positive* impression. All of this was driven by Millennials using social media's word-of-mouth power.

DECISION MAKING

As we age, the way we like to make decisions changes. We tend to become more trusting, prefer fewer options, and rely more heavily on intuition. A white paper released by the Cornell University College of Ecology makes the case:

> When it comes to choice in decision-making, the contemporary mentality seems typified by a more-is-better mantra. But is this the case for all individuals? Research

by Dr. Mikels and Dr. Simon suggests that while such a mentality may be part of the exuberance of youth, older adults neither desire, nor value, choice to the same extent that younger adults do (Reed, Mikels, and Simon 2008).

In a series of large-scale surveys conducted in Ithaca and New York City, hundreds of older adults (over 65) and undergraduate students reported how many options they wished to choose from in a variety of domains, from prescription drug plans to ice cream flavors. As expected, older adults desired on average less than half as many options as younger adults did, and this preference for choice continued to decline even among the oldest participants. That is, not only did the average 70-year-old desire fewer options than a 20-year-old, but 80-year-olds desired even fewer options than 70-year-olds.[1]

For companies that target the older affluent, this means altering your messages. The Cornell article also reports that adults not only want fewer options, but they also make better decisions when fewer options are presented and they're happier with those decisions. In sum, older affluent consumers want trustworthy salespeople to simplify the decision-making process.

Let's say you're working with an affluent client in her seventies. Whether she's in the market for new kitchen, luxury automobile, or estate-planning attorney, she probably doesn't want a laundry list of options or six people to call. Give her one (possibly two) experts to consider and then *introduce* her to these professionals.

---

[1] Andrew E. Reed, "Hearts, Minds, and Choices: Helping Improve Decision-Making Across the Life Span," Department of Human Development, Cornell University. Retrieved from www.human.cornell.edu/hd/outreach-extension/loader.cfm?csModule =security/getfile&PageID=43529.

The Millennials and Generation X may appear difficult with all of their digital research, but this the new normal. They are information savvy but, in many ways, knowledge deficient. Though they conduct copious online research, they often need guidance when it's time to take action. They are also sensitive about any perceived condescension tied to their youth (e.g., "After you've seen a few recessions you'll understand how it impacts the real estate market").

A conversation with a colleague about his daughter's recent house purchase paints a clear picture. Her profile is typical of the emerging affluent: a 28-year-old professional with an MBA, married, owner of a starter home. Her husband is two years older with a similar profile. Both are high-income Millennials who qualify as emerging affluent.

They were on a family vacation at the beach when the daughter (Anne) peeked at her smartphone and said, "Dad, take a look at this house. It just came on the market. It's in the right neighborhood and within our price range. What do you think?"

After a brief conversation, my colleague discovered that his daughter had been doing a lot of research, knew the local housing market, and could afford the purchase. His only advice was to make an appointment with the Realtor, and if the house checked out, make a serious offer immediately. Apparently, this voice of experience was the nudge the couple needed. Anne contacted the Realtor (a friend) and scheduled an appointment for the next day. All of this was done via text, sitting under an umbrella at the beach.

The house met expectations, so the couple made a serious offer before a Realtor's sign had even been placed in the yard. (The house had been shown seven times in the two days it was on the market.) Less than 24 hours later, the offer was accepted by the seller.

This is a glimpse into how a $435,000 home was purchased by a Millennial couple. It's a glimpse into how the emerging affluent do business.

Things to Keep in Mind	
Younger Clients/Prospects	**Older Clients/Prospects**
More options	Fewer options
Rely on analytical skills	Rely on their "gut instincts"
Digital research	Word-of-mouth (keep things simple)
Text, email	Face-to-face, telephone
Information heavy	Selective information
Price aware	Value aware (price transparency)
Experience deficient (don't know what they don't know)	Experienced (know what they don't know)
Social media users	Growing awareness of social media

Imagine if Anne had an experienced Realtor, someone her father had known over the years, who understood real estate but didn't understand the generational communication differences. Would a Saturday afternoon text lead to an immediate showing?

Anne discovered the house through digital research. She knew the market, was price savvy, and texted to schedule the appointment. What if her father hadn't encouraged her to follow her instincts and act quickly? She might have acted, or she might have missed the opportunity—in which case, all of her digital research would have been for naught.

Understanding how this generation communicates will help you develop a rapport on *their* terms and ultimately help them to make better decisions.

COMMUNICATION

One walk through the supermarket reveals how much communication styles vary by age. The younger generations send a constant stream of texts, tweets, and Facebook posts. Ten years ago, nobody did these things. Today, they're considered mainstream communication.

Chances are that many of your best clients, prospects, and centers of influence are a few years removed from the aforementioned texting/tweeting crowd. This older generation grew up with letters, phone calls, and personal visits. Some have transitioned to the new technology faster than others, but most seniors still prefer personal methods of communication.

Our affluent research is very clear on which communications media the affluent prefer for complex interactions, which includes major purchases:

- Face-to-face   71%
- Telephone   15%
- Email   7%

This might appear to contradict Anne's texting. However, she got on the phone with the Realtor as soon as she left the beach. Thereafter, her communication consisted of an in-person tour of the house. Obviously, Anne's Realtor was able to communicate with her on her level to set the appointment. This led to the telephone and then to personal interaction.

Another takeaway from Anne's case is the responsiveness of the Realtor. She not only communicated immediately by text to schedule the showing, but answered Anne's preliminary questions over the phone, showed the house, and presented the offer in the span of just 18 hours. I'm told this same Realtor is listing Anne's current house, and even though Anne is the one who found the new house, Anne is likely to initiate positive word-of-mouth influence on the Realtor's behalf because of the excellent service she provided.

We know that personalized communication and responsiveness have a positive correlation with client loyalty, positive word-of-mouth influence, and referrals/personal introductions. This holds true for every generation of affluent consumers. To put it mildly, it's important to be responsive with clients and prospects.

GENERATIONAL SIMILARITIES

As purchases become higher in value, and more hard-earned dollars are required, the younger generations become eerily similar to their senior brethren. Younger people also solicit the opinions of people they respect and trust; the quality of the salesperson is very important to them; and all of the expectations displayed by older (demanding and skeptical) affluent consumers rise to the surface. See the following regarding what's important to *all* affluent consumers:

Important in Initial Major Purchase Search
- Personal inspection or consultation
- Online research
- Word-of-mouth influence (opinions and recommendations)

Important in Making Final Major Purchase Decision
- Product or service meets needs
- Trust that the product or service is as advertised (promised)
- Reputation of the company

Factors in Repeat Purchase
- Good service
- Problems resolved quickly
- Warranty

Don't take a one-size-fits-all approach to communications. The secret is getting to know your clients and then communicating in the ways they prefer. This means:

- *Stay current.* This doesn't necessarily mean setting up a Twitter account, but if your younger clients and prospects are heavily into text messaging, it helps to understand and use that technology.
- *Open the dialogue.* Asking clients and prospects how they like to communicate with you is a great way to initiate and maintain

a great back and forth. Emailing a client who doesn't email is a slow way to do business. I've known people who so rarely check their email that it would be faster to deliver messages to them by hand—even if they live thousands of miles away.

- *Be responsive.* Staying current with technology and knowing people's preferred communications media is only helpful if you're responsive. You have to be dialed into their timeline, not yours. How responsive? Very. As fast as possible.

- *Protect your online brand.* You definitely want to make a good first impression when prospects like Anne are conducting online research. When it comes to your online presence, ask yourself: "Does my site provide helpful information? Is it easy to navigate? Does it feature a professional look? Are key social media sites linked to it? Does it help accelerate the major purchase decision?"

- *Monitor your competition online.* Are you aware of what clients and prospects are seeing when they search for your services online? Where do you rank in a Google search? What is your competition offering? The younger generation is information heavy. The last thing you want is for them to acquire more knowledge than you.

SUMMARY

The key to understanding the generational divide is to remember a few ground rules. The first of these is: One communications medium doesn't fit all.

The emerging affluent are a major economic force. They're coming, with spending power that will soon earn many of them affluent status. In addition, they will inherit far more of their money than any previous generation in recorded history.

Research Facts
- Twenty percent of households earning $100,000 or more are Millennials (ages 18 to 30).

- Thirty-three percent of households earning $100,000 or more are Generation X (ages 31 to 46).
- Thirty-three percent of households earning $100,000 or more are Baby Boomers (ages 47 to 66).
- Our APD research tells us that 95 percent of all consumers conduct online research as they being their quest for a major purchase.
- Face-to-face is the preferred communication mode for complex transactions (major purchase decisions) with affluent consumers of all generations.
- Fifty percent of Millennials check their email and Facebook pages within 30 minutes of waking.
- Smartphones and tablets are becoming commonplace across all generations of affluence.

Taking Action

- Identify the profile of your affluent client base. You will likely discover that most of your interactions are with one segment or another.
- Honestly assess your preferred communication style as it compares with the profile of your typical affluent client.
- Learn how to adjust your communication to each generation: fewer options and more simplicity for seniors, more options and more information for Millennials.
- Review your online presence and make necessary adjustments for professionalism, clarity, detailed information, ease of use, and prominence in Google searches.
- Review the online presence of your competition.
- Make certain you are current on digital communication basics: online research, smartphones, tablets, and so forth.

Chapter 9   The Amazon Effect

Ninety-five percent of affluent consumers perform online research before making a major purchase decision.
                              —Factoid, 2013 APD Research

A few years ago, my wife gave me permission to upgrade the flat-screen television in our living room. Her instructions were simple: "I don't think we need a bigger television, but if you *do* get one, it better match the aesthetics of the room. The fireplace [over which the screen had been professionally mounted] had better not turn into one big television."

After receiving the green light, my first reaction was a silent "Thank you!" My second was to call my brother, an early adopter of electronic toys.

During the call, he shared his knowledge of flat-screen technology and told me how to perform some online research. This initial online search led to three top-rated models approved by my brother/consultant. I was almost ready to make the purchase, but I wanted to see these televisions in person.

Unfortunately, my forays into the brick-and-mortar world proved disappointing. Circuit City didn't carry the models I wanted, and there were few salespeople available to assist me. (In hindsight, we all know why.) The trip was a waste of my time.

Best Buy had plenty of salespeople, but nothing else that would prompt me to stimulate positive word-of-mouth in affluent circles. The store advertised one of the models, but it wasn't in stock. (Huh?) And instead of ordering the model, the salesperson pressured me to choose another one. He supplied copious quantities of unsolicited information about a unit I didn't want. Within minutes, he became so pushy that I made a lame excuse to flee the store. It was another waste of time, and an irritating one to boot.

I shared these frustrations with my brother and, to my surprise, he suggested I try Amazon.com. What an eye-opening experience! Not only did Amazon have my favorite model, but the price was better than Best Buy's and it included delivery and installation of the unit by an "Amazon-approved" technician. In under a week, I was the proud owner of a new 60-inch flat-screen television. Just as important, my wife approved.

I didn't know it at the time, but I had just been influenced by the *Amazon Effect*—one of several increasingly important factors that affect the purchase decisions of affluent consumers. These factors include:

- *The gender shift:* Among today's affluent, the female of the household is extremely influential when it comes to major financial, purchase, and investment decisions. (I required my wife's permission before buying the new TV, and this permission was conditional: The final product had to match her interior design specs.)

- *Word-of-mouth influence: Buzz* has become a major factor in how the affluent make purchase decisions. Their increasing distrust of advertising messages, combined with their skeptical nature, is driving them to put more emphasis on the opinions and recommendations of people they trust and respect. (After getting permission from my wife, my next step was to phone my brother for advice and recommendations.)

- *Online research:* Ninety-five percent of affluent consumers conduct online research to guide their decision making. They read online reviews and pay close attention to the details and overall quality of the reviews. (Following my brother's advice, I went online to research flat-screen TVs, learning more than I needed to know.)

- *The Amazon Effect:* Like me, many affluent consumers turn to sites such as Amazon.com to start their research, but end up making purchases there. In my case, Amazon offered the right product, supplied enough information to help me make an informed decision, and the price was right. Amazon also offered value-added benefits.

- *Convenience/ease of purchase:* The Amazon transaction was much easier and far more pleasant than my brick-and-mortar encounters. Since Amazon already had my personal information on file (from earlier book purchases), my only task was being available for delivery and installation. Today's affluent want hassle-free shopping experiences, as do many nonaffluent shoppers. A recent survey of 7,000 consumers reveals that the biggest factor influencing the decision to actually purchase (and to recommend a product/service) is "the ease with which [they] can gather trustworthy information about a product and confidently and efficiently weigh their purchase options."[1]

Has the Amazon Effect served a death warrant to every salesperson? No. That warrant will be issued *only* to those who fail to adapt to the new market realities—to salespeople who refuse to retool to satisfy the needs and wants of the affluent. The Amazon Effect will also spell doom to companies whose products and services don't deliver on their promises.

It's all about trust. Whether you're an online retailer or a brick-and-mortar service provider, if your target market is the affluent, building trust is the essential first step. Building trust requires that you understand the target's needs. It requires that you display empathy by taking a personal interest in those needs. It requires that you take action to meet the needs.

When it comes to the Amazon Effect, the good news is that meeting the needs and expectations of the affluent is best accomplished via face-to-face encounters and real-world relationships. The bad news is that the Amazon Effect has raised the expectations of the affluent vis-à-vis convenience, speed, and simplicity.

Already, Millennials and Generation Xers are arriving in stores equipped with Amazon apps on their iPhones. They're pulling your items from the shelves, scanning bar codes with these handy-dandy apps, and (voilà!) making real-time price comparisons. Because brick and mortar retailers must now compete with online discounters, they must not only show greater sensitivity to pricing but do a better job of managing relationships with affluent customers.

---

[1] Patrick Spenner and Karen Freeman, "To Keep Your Customers, Keep It Simple," *Harvard Business Review*, May 2012.

To put this into context, let's examine the top-five factors that influence affluent consumers' major purchase decisions—in order of importance:

1. Product or service meets their needs.
2. They trust the product or service will deliver as advertised.
3. Reputation of the company.
4. Warranty.
5. Ease of returning/refund.

Among upscale consumers, finding the lowest price ranked seventh in importance (below responsiveness of the sales and service personnel), whereas finding the lowest price ranked second among the nonaffluent. Yes, the affluent are different. Yes, they will sometimes haggle about price, but they *will* pay a fair price in exchange for real value. (Please note, however, that trust and reputation are a part of their value equation.)

Can a retailer with a broad spectrum of affluent and nonaffluent clients (such as a sporting goods store) segment its client base by annual purchase dollars? Yes, if it makes the effort. This type of segmentation is no different than what airlines do with frequent flyer programs, giving preferential treatment to customers who spend more. If companies like Amazon and L.L. Bean can recommend items based on past purchases, so can physical retailers. In fact, physical retailers could do a *better* job if they leveraged their personal relationships with these customers.

THE APPLE EXPERIENCE

Apple's physical stores have set the standard for convenience and personal attention. Visit any Apple store, and you'll see it bustling with people. Many customers are older and affluent. Many are members of the Millennial and Generation X crowd. What all of them have in common is a willingness to spend top dollar for the "Apple Experience." What's going on?

The secret to the "Apple Experience" is personal service. You are personally greeted on entering the store. From there, you're assigned a personal Apple staffer, a noncommissioned salesperson who's both knowledgeable and a good communicator. The staffer is skilled at asking and answering questions, can provide quick tutorials when necessary, and can even conduct the entire transaction via iPhone.

The Apple Experience began with the opening of Apple's flagship store in Manhattan, which occurred just as Gateway Computers was closing its retail stores. Since then, the Apple Experience has contributed to the demise of Dell computers, which was once the dominant force in online computer sales.

Today's affluent market is bifurcated, with Amazon on one side and Apple on the other. Both companies generate tremendous revenues from affluent consumers. The secret for *your* success is to mirror the Apple Experience while adjusting to the Amazon Effect.

ONLINE RESEARCH

One of the biggest trends affecting consumer behavior is online research. The chart below reveals how prevalent online research has become in every demographic category. Seventy-two percent of nonaffluent consumers and 95 percent of the affluent claim to "occasionally or always" conduct online research before making a purchase.

Online Search for a Provider	Nonaffluent	Affluent
Always search online	29%	39%
Occasionally search online	43%	56%
Never search online	28%	5%

Since only 5 percent of affluent respondents tell us that they never search online, it's wise to assume that online research will continue to grow. (By the way, the larger the purchase, the more research the affluent will conduct in advance.)

When was the last time you read an online review? I just finished a movie review to determine whether I should download a movie to my iPad for an upcoming flight. Online reviews are often helpful, but not always. In 2012, Amazon earned widespread scorn when it was discovered that some authors solicited favorable reviews from friends and family for their literary masterworks and, in other cases, hired paid reviewers to heap praise on their books and savage the competition. Unfortunately, Amazon's solution was a partial one:

> Giving raves to family members is no longer acceptable. Neither is writers' reviewing other writers. But showering five stars on a book you admittedly have not read is fine.
>
> After several well-publicized cases involving writers buying or manipulating their reviews, Amazon is cracking down. Writers say thousands of reviews have been deleted from the shopping site in recent months.
>
> Amazon has not said how many reviews it has killed, nor has it offered any public explanation. So its sweeping but hazy purge has generated an uproar about what it means to review in an era when everyone is an author and everyone is a reviewer.[2]

Why all the "uproar" over online reviews? Because many consumers trust online reviewers to be impartial arbiters of what's worth buying and what's not.

This uproar has gotten so loud that at the time of this writing the *New York Times* ran an update on the dishonest review theme.

> New York regulators will announce on Monday the most comprehensive crackdown on deceptive reviews on the Internet. Agreements have been reached with 19 companies to cease their misleading practice and pay a total of $350,000 in penalties.

---

[2]David Streitfeld, "Giving Mom's Book Five Stars? Amazon May Cull Your Review," *New York Times*, December 22, 2012.

This yearlong investigation encompassed companies that create fake reviews as well as the clients who buy them. Among those signing the agreements are a charter bus operator, a teeth-whitening service, a laser hair-removal chain, and an adult entertainment club. Also signing are several reputation-enhancement firms that place fraudulent reviews on sites like Google, Yelp, Citysearch, and Yahoo.[3]

As such, reviews and reviewers have a major impact on purchase decisions and are now becoming accountable for their authenticity. While it's important to recognize that reviews are important to the decision-making process, it's even more important to determine *why* some reviews are considered helpful and others aren't, and to pinpoint the type of information the affluent consider most helpful.

Most Helpful with Online Reviews	Nonaffluent	Affluent
Details in the review	30%	37%
Quality of the review	19%	33%
Insights from negative reviews	12%	10%
Source of the review	7%	10%
Do not use online reviews	13%	6%
Use multiple reviews	20%	4%

As the saying goes, "The devil is in the details." It is the *quality* of the review that determines whether the affluent, more than the nonaffluent, will find the review helpful.

What does any of this have to do with selling to the affluent? Everything!

Even as online shopping becomes the norm, the affluent are seeking *human interaction*—human insights, opinions, and experiences—to help them make major decisions.

The medical field is one example of this "bipolar" approach to shopping.

---

[3]David Streitfeld, "Give Yourself 5 Stars? Online, It Might Cost You," *New York Times*, September 22, 2013.

For a decade, physicians have been encountering more and more self-diagnosed patients—people who research their symptoms on sites like WebMD before scheduling visits. This research hasn't made the family physician obsolete. Instead, it's helped consumers become more knowledgeable about a wide range of illnesses and conditions, prompting some people to visit their doctor, whereas before they might have dismissed the symptoms. (On the minus side, self-diagnosis tends to cause annoyance among doctors, especially when the diagnosis is faulty or the patient is a hypochondriac.) The bottom line: Although more consumers perform online research, nobody is trying to obtain medical treatment online.

Today's affluent want to know their options in advance, so the Amazon Effect is forcing companies to pay closer attention to clients' needs and expectations. It's forcing them to take a more personal approach with clients and develop value propositions to justify their prices.

Online giants and specialty companies alike should be thinking beyond algorithms. They should be getting more personal with their customers. In addition to tracking the latest products that clients have viewed, merchants should maintain databases of personal information on each buyer. The database should include information ranging from buyers' names and spouses' names to the number and ages of their children, travel patterns, favorite books and music, and so forth.

Armed with this knowledge, online retailers can personalize their greetings and other messages, and even ask personal questions. Is this the same as interacting with a professional who's mastered the art of affluent selling? No. But it can further personalize the online shopping experience. (It's no different than when the affluent visit their doctors. Before the visit, the patient will conduct a little research before deciding whether to contact the doctor.) The net result is that shoppers become better informed before seeking personal advice and guidance from a customer service rep or salesperson, but this doesn't mean that customer service reps and salespeople will become obsolete. Far from it!

The following chart reveals what the affluent value most when starting the purchase process.

Importance for Initial Search	
Personal inspection/consultation	89%
Online research	83%
Opinions/recommendations	63%
Information in periodicals	52%

With "personal inspection" ranking first in importance, it would behoove every product and service provider to make a good first impression. Every merchant, salesperson, and customer service representative must strive to provide the *antithesis* of my flat-screen-TV experience. Nothing turns off an affluent shopper faster than misleading ads and pushy salespeople.

Please note that the information in the chart above can also be applied to services, as a friend's experience with a carpet installer will show.

Dan and Laura have a large house with a fully carpeted upstairs. Laura thought the carpet was looking worn and wanted to replace it. This prompted Dan to launch a search for replacement carpeting. First, he talked with a neighbor who'd recently recarpeted his upstairs. The neighbor recommended the same company he had hired. Next, Dan went online and found another local company, one whose history and website made a good first impression.

Dan contacted both companies, visited their showrooms to view samples, and scheduled a time for reps from both companies to measure his upstairs and prepare proposals. At this point in the search, Dan and Laura weren't leaning toward either company. But the proposals sealed the deal. Both reps spent considerable time measuring the upstairs and the stairway, and the following day, one rep emailed a detailed written proposal.

"We were going to spend close to $10,000 on carpeting," said Dan. "Both companies seemed reputable, and I wanted two quotes. But after a week of not hearing from the other carpet rep,

I called . . . and I couldn't believe the response. He told me he'd already *given* me a quote—the ballpark guesstimate he provided after he finished measuring. I *specifically* told him to put that estimate into a written proposal!"

Needless to say, Dan and Laura chose the company that delivered the written proposal. It just so happened that this was the company the neighbor recommended. The installation was seamless, and Dan and Laura even received a follow-up call from the company's owner a week later to see if everything was okay.

Not only did one company botch a $10,000 opportunity, they also stimulated negative word-of-mouth influence. Do you think Dan and Laura will recount their experience within their spheres of influence? You bet they will! That's how I heard the story. One carpet company got the business and will benefit from positive word-of-mouth influence; the other received scathing reviews and still doesn't have a clue what went wrong.

What does this have to do with the Amazon Effect?

Dan's online search led him to an established company that made a good first impression. The transaction wasn't completed online, but it was *initiated* online. Had this company not made a good online impression, it would never have been considered. Had the company made a good *second* impression, it might have gotten the job.

Although the Amazon Effect has a powerful influence on consumer behavior, it can't compensate for boneheaded mistakes, arrogance, and poor customer service. Conversely, personalized service and active listening can sometimes overcome a poor web presence, or no web presence at all.

A few years ago, my friend Paul learned that his home's heating and air conditioning system needed repairs. He learned this after an inspection from the company with which he had an extended service contract. After getting the diagnosis, Paul scheduled an appointment with a company salesperson. Unfortunately, this guy turned out to be the kind of salesman who gives the word "cheesy" a bad name. (Let's call him "Dexter.")

From the beginning, Paul explained that he was interested *only* in repairing what was broken, not purchasing a whole new system. Dexter ignored this request and spent the next hour holding Paul hostage to a poorly scripted sales presentation. First, Dexter insisted on walking Paul through a stack of brochures as part of his canned presentation. Next, he continually stressed the "benefits" of various gold- and platinum-level HVAC systems in which Paul had *no* interest. Finally, he attempted to rush Paul into signing a contract on the spot, promising him a modest discount if the papers were signed within 12 hours.

"Dexter was like a character from a David Mamet play," said Paul. "His approach was an exercise in slick, depersonalized service. At one point, he even pulled the old high-pressure stunt of 'calling the boss' to see if he'd reduce the price. Price was never the issue! Most of my system was brand new, and I didn't want to replace perfectly good equipment, which is what Dexter was trying to get me to do."

Paul was so incensed that he refused to buy a thing from the company, ever. Instead, he got exactly what he wanted from another firm—one he found in an old-fashioned phone book. (The company has no website.)

This company's salesman ("Gerry") initiated the conversation by asking Paul what *he* wanted. He listened patiently, took notes, and responded to Paul's questions with terse, straightforward answers. No gimmicks. No pressure. No BS.

Gerry told Paul he could easily repair the damaged system with replacement units priced from A through Z, and responded with specific answers to Paul's questions. The whole transaction was done in less than 20 minutes.

Gerry made the sale, and he made it look effortless.

It *should* have been effortless. Paul was anxious to fix his home's HVAC system before the weather turned cold. It's not like he had much choice about having the system fixed. Truth be told, Gerry may or may not be an amazing salesman. But he *is* a good listener. Because he responded to the customer's questions and concerns, he didn't have to stage a theatrical sales presentation to win the business. He merely had to treat Paul like a human being.

That's what the affluent want: convenience, trustworthy information, and highly personalized service.

SUMMARY

When today's affluent undertake a major purchase, their search will usually involve a combination of personal inspection, consultations, online research, solicitation of opinions and recommendations from friends and family, and a search through periodicals. All are important, but since 95 percent conduct online research, the Amazon Effect is ubiquitous. What's more, the Amazon Effect will continue to grow, and as it grows, the importance of affluent sales mastery will grow. The affluent expect personalized attention as part of the sales process.

The Apple Experience counterbalances the Amazon Effect. It illustrates the power of personal experience, a knowledgeable and friendly staff, an easy transaction process, strong service, and an excellent reputation. Word-of-mouth influence plays a major role in the purchase process, whether that influence takes the form of online reviews, a great purchasing experience, or a negative experience with a particular merchant or product.

To sell to the affluent, you need to mirror the Apple Experience while recognizing and adapting to the Amazon Effect.

Research Facts

- Ninety-five percent of the affluent conduct online research before making a major purchase decision, and 72 percent of the nonaffluent do so as well.
- The number one factor affecting a major purchase decision is whether the product or service meets the buyer's needs.
- The second factor affecting a major purchase decision is whether the buyer trusts that the product or service will be as advertised.

- The third factor in a major purchase decision is reputation of the company.
- The affluent focus on two areas when using reviews: 37 percent consider "detail" in review to be the most helpful, while 33 percent believe the "quality" of the review is the most important thing.
- Only 6 percent of today's affluent don't read online reviews.
- Eighty-nine percent of the affluent consider "personal inspection/consultation" as the most important factor in their initial search.

Taking Action

- Put yourself in an affluent consumer's shoes by conducting an online search for your product/service.
- Make sure your website creates a good first impression, and be aware what kind of impression your competitors' websites make.
- Assess the transaction process for your product or service. Make sure it's as fast and convenient as possible.
- Make an effort to deliver personalized service to every affluent prospect. Review your initial greeting in order to mirror the Apple Experience.
- Review your follow-up procedures. You'll want to conduct personal follow-ups with every major purchaser to help stimulate word-of-mouth influence.
- Truth in advertising is essential to affluent decision making. Make sure your products and services perform just as promised.

Chapter 10 How to Move Upmarket

Annual household spending by the affluent is nearly six times greater than that of nonaffluent households.
                    —Factoid, 2013 APD Research

When the notorious bank robber Willy Sutton was asked why he targeted banks, he allegedly replied, "That's where the money is." That sentiment should be memorized by every salesperson to the affluent: "I sell to upscale consumers because that's where the money is."

Every sales professional wants to collect larger commission checks by acquiring a loyal, affluent clientele. But how does one move upmarket? How does one succeed where so many others have failed or continue to struggle? The answer to that question is literally worth a billion dollars. It's been estimated that over $1 billion in commissions is left on the table each year by salespeople struggling to move upmarket.

A couple of years ago, a psychologist attended one of our two-day boot camps to learn about the affluent sales process. After the first day's sessions, she pulled me aside and whispered, "As a clinically trained psychologist, let me tell you the biggest challenge facing these participants in mastering the art of affluent sales: fear."

She was right. Fear of rejection, fear of failure, fear of embarrassment, fear of being perceived as stupid—the list of fears is endless.

A few years ago, my firm was asked to train a division of an international conglomerate's sales force on the art of affluent sales. This division sold home and office security systems to protect against fire, break-ins, and so forth. Their new focus: luxury homes in the $1 million or greater range. After taking a hard look into the future, their executive committee recognized that the digital world offered a tremendous opportunity for marketing high-tech security systems to affluent homeowners. After all, these people own second (and sometimes third) homes. Couple this with today's economic climate, the ongoing war on terrorism, and the 24/7 media drumbeat of fear, and today's affluent have become extremely security conscious.

Sounds like a natural fit, doesn't it? A world leader in the home/business security business goes upmarket. The company invests millions to develop cutting-edge digital security devices that interface with the electronics found in most affluent homes, nurturing a new and extremely profitable market.

Well . . . not so fast.

By the time this company contacted my firm, they were about a year into the roll-out of the new division. Though I wouldn't characterize their call as "panicked," they were definitely concerned. I flew to their headquarters to ask questions and listen. Because a lot had been invested, a lot was expected. I sensed a degree of discomfort among those still aligned with the core business model—a model that was successful, profitable, and being used to fund the new division. These dynamics had a direct influence on the company's sales training.

Noted for excellent training of their core-model sales force, this global firm was now attempting to train the new corps of salespeople with a slightly modified version of the original sales training. Unfortunately, the program was conducted by former salespeople who didn't truly understand affluent sales.

Their first mistake was teaching recruits to use a canned dialog featuring the timeworn three-option menu (a technique that usually prompts buyers to select the mid-priced option). This dialog serves only to *annoy* most affluent buyers.

The second, third, and fourth mistakes all stemmed from ignorance of the fear factor and its potential impact.

Every member of the new sales corps had made a good living selling cameras and motion detectors priced from $250 to $500. These nationally advertised products were the subjects of price wars with competitors, so sales often depended on price. This was the world in which the recruits had been groomed. This was the world in which they felt comfortable. This was the world in which they excelled. They were good at selling price-sensitive commodity products to nonaffluent customers. They could naturally relate to price-sensitive consumers.

But now they were being asked to conduct onsite needs analyses with affluent home owners. The onsite visits were part of a multistep process of selling a hybrid product that combined high-tech features with prices ranging from $5,000 to $20,000 or more. The recently knighted sales force couldn't relate, and couldn't cope. They couldn't imagine anyone spending that kind of money on a security system for their home. With few exceptions, the elite sales force was suffering from an acute case of intimidation. They were afraid of moving upmarket.

However, this fear could be overcome, and it became the basis of our training with the hand-selected sales force in the newly formed luxury home division. I'll spare you all the details. Suffice it to say that we introduced the fine art of selling to the affluent during our workshops, which helped the team break free of previous attitudes and inappropriate sales techniques. We taught them how to create good first impressions in terms of personal dress and the cleanliness of their vehicles; taught them to develop a rapport and to ask the right questions in a conversational (yet professional) manner; taught them how to involve affluent prospects in a needs analysis of their homes' security systems; and, most important, deep-sixed the antiquated three-option proposals. The new sales force learned to develop personal relationships with prospective clients, creating proposals based on *real needs*. Ultimately, this made it easier to clinch deals and form long-term relationships.

In some respects we "rewired" each salesperson by undoing the sales training they had received over the years. Simultaneously, we sold them on the idea that they, too, could become affluent— by selling to the affluent. Without this internal sale, very few salespeople allow themselves to venture far from their comfort zones. However, once salespeople recognize that their *personal* fast track to affluence lies in mastering affluent sales, they allow themselves to feel the fear before letting it slip away.

Success is also contagious. Within two months of our initial workshop, one of luxury home security reps made the largest home-security sale in company history. Granted, it was in Beverly Hills, but the rep had developed a relationship with the buyer, who was charged with handling the estate of a Hollywood star who was obsessed with privacy and security. One step led to another, and after a careful onsite analysis with the star's handler, the salesman's proposal became a scheduled installation.

This sale wasn't the tipping point for the sales team. It was so big that initially it was hard for other reps to wrap their heads around it. But it *was* the beginning. As more affluent success stories poured in, the issue of being intimidated by moving upmarket faded into the past.

AMERICA ON $250,000 A YEAR

It's important to recognize the nature of your affluent clients and prospects.

When President Obama defined wealth (for tax purposes) as households with annual incomes of $250,000, affluence became a hot topic in many circles. One reason this definition became such a lightning-rod campaign issue is that most members of the quarter-million-dollar club do *not* perceive themselves as wealthy.

In his blog *The Wealth Report*, Robert Frank's post "Struggling on $350,000 a Year"[1] cited two examples of this attitude. An attorney and a financial marketing executive, earning $250,000 and $350,000 respectively, complained that they were barely scraping by (although the marketing executive confessed to spending $32,000 a year on his daughter's private school). "The blog ignited a new class battle on the web," said Dexter. The attorney "was virulently attacked on the web as a 'rich whiner.'"

The battle between the haves and have-nots is nothing new. Nor is it our concern. What *is* our concern is the mind-set of the affluent.

---

[1] Robert Frank, "'Struggling' on $350,00 a Year," *Wall Street Journal*, February 29, 2012.

Much like most readers of this book, whatever the size and nature of their purchases, most of the affluent consider themselves middle class. The vast majority hail from middle-class backgrounds and have not shed that identity. Because very few have inherited their wealth and have worked hard to acquire their money, they don't put themselves in the same category as the "idle rich."

Based on our criteria of $250,000 in annual household income or $500,000 in investable assets, 94 percent of affluent males and 91 percent of affluent females are currently in the workforce. Twenty-one percent of affluent males own their own businesses versus 7 percent of affluent females; 23 percent of affluent men are self-employed versus 11 percent of females; 50 percent of affluent men earn employee salaries or commission versus 73 percent of affluent females.

	Affluent	Men	Women
Salary/commission as employee	59%	50%	73%
Self-employed professional	18%	23%	11%
Business ownership	16%	21%	7%
Inheritance	2%	2%	4%
Investment/Property	2%	2%	1%
Disability/social security	1%	1%	1%
Retirement	1%	2%	0%

(Due to rounding, the numbers do not add up to 100.)

Today's affluent were raised to get a good education, work hard, and better themselves. They don't perceive themselves as affluent, but as striving members of the vast and upwardly mobile middle. It is vital, therefore, that you never patronize these people by labeling them affluent, wealthy, or rich—not to their faces. If you use such terms in their presence, you're likely to offend them.

THE WORKING AFFLUENT

Not only are the affluent working, they are working *hard*. If you work hard, too, they respect you. Affluent men work longer hours than their female counterparts: 68 percent work 40 to 59 hours a week, compared with 46 percent of affluent females. This is not to imply that affluent women aren't as hardworking as men. Eighty-five percent are married, which may explain why they work fewer hours in a given week. Many have domestic responsibilities that range from shuttling the kids to day care and sports activities to grocery shopping and meal preparation.

As you'll see in the following chart, affluent women spend a lot of time working. And guess what? They *know* they work hard, which is one reason they expect no less from someone who provides services and products. They expect the same level of professionalism and the same depth and breadth of knowledge that they strive to provide. In addition, they insist on receiving this professionalism within the context of a pleasant experience.

Hours Worked per Week	Men	Women
1 to 39 hours	12%	26%
40 to 59 hours	68%	46%
60 to 69 hours	4%	6%
70 hours or more	0%	1%
Retired	14%	11%
Unemployed	2%	8%

When you look at the source of wealth and number of hours worked per week, it becomes evident that you are probably very much like your affluent prospects. They are not to be feared. Overall, we have found that to successfully move upmarket, three criteria must be addressed; mind-set, knowledge, and upmarket opportunity. (These are important to salespeople, but also to sales managers when they are interviewing candidates who will be selling upmarket.)

MIND-SET

A major impediment that confronts almost all salespeople is their mind-set. The seven inches of gray matter between the ears often act as a speed bump to earnings potential.

Following a recent lecture, one attendee approached me and said, "I just wanted to thank you. I read *The Art of Selling to the Affluent*, followed your teachings, and have tripled my income over the past four years." I had just challenged the audience to think in terms of doubling their income. This might sound a bit pie-in-the-sky, but it's common among salespeople who *give themselves permission* to move upmarket. This rep said his biggest challenge was giving himself permission to go for it—to concentrate on the affluent. He had to *believe* (without evidence) that he could succeed in moving upmarket.

Before you do anything else, you must make your most important sale: to yourself. It's essential that you reverse engineer this process in your mind—that you imagine your lifestyle five years from now after mastering the art of affluent salesmanship. Nobody can do this for you.

Consider the benefits of moving upmarket. Are the rewards worth the mental and physical effort? Few salespeople succeed in moving upmarket without first closing this internal deal.

Note to sales managers: Just because someone can sell, doesn't mean he or she will be successful in selling upmarket. You must determine whether the salesperson is made of the right stuff. Aside from having the person read this book, you'll want to assess the following:

- *Goal focus.* Is the candidate serious about significantly increasing his or her income? Ask for a three-year lifestyle projection, and get as much detail as possible.
- *Toughness.* Does the candidate have a thick enough skin to deal with the skeptical/cynical affluent? We've found it helpful to role play with each candidate using two scenarios: an initial meeting with a prospect and dealing with an upset client. Whenever you

employ role playing during an interview, ask a third party to participate so you can focus on evaluating the results.

- *Presence.* It's easier to teach someone how to dress than to teach him or her personal presence. Presence is a mind-set. You want people who believe in themselves.

KNOWLEDGE

As an affluent sales professional, your role is that of a consultant. Affluent consumers expect you to assist them in making major purchase decisions. To do this, you need a thorough knowledge of your products and/or services, and you must have the ability to communicate this in user-friendly ways. Don't get lost in the black hole of "features and benefits." Many salespeople think they're impressing prospects by showcasing their technical expertise when they're doing precisely the opposite—losing the sale. You must do more than memorize a list of features and benefits. You must know how to *persuade.* You must showcase your industry expertise, discussing the strengths and weaknesses of your competitors, alternatives to your products or services, and ways in which your wares better address the needs and wants of affluent prospects. This expertise demands a passion that goes beyond day-to-day salesmanship. It demands that you always reside in "learning mode."

Note to sales managers: It's important that an affluent sales candidate be curious and open to learning. Usually, a healthy learning curve is associated with any upmarket product or service, and you'll want your candidates to embrace the challenge of climbing that curve. Curiosity signals a thirst for knowledge. This is the hallmark of salespeople who are willing to study the industry on their own time and research the competition, including their products and services, strengths and weaknesses, and web presence.

In part, the interview should focus on the candidate's knowledge of the industry, the competition, and the options available to affluent consumers other than your products or services.

OPPORTUNITY

It's not unusual for sales professionals to believe they have no opportunities to move upmarket even when opportunities are staring them in the face.

Whether it's the home security salesperson who decides to focus on securing homes in the $750,000 price range, or the financial planner who focuses on families with $1 million or more in investable assets, opportunities abound to move upmarket.

Many salespeople have a blind spot for upmarket opportunities because they look to the future with one eye focused on the rearview mirror. They focus on what they've always done. They focus on current clients, and those to whom they've sold in the past. This blinds them to upmarket opportunities. We hear it all time: "There isn't a lot of money in this area." "People won't spend money on a financial plan." "Million-dollar homes aren't selling." And the beat goes on.

In our experience, once affluent sales antennae are activated, upmarket opportunities will appear from nowhere. If they don't, find a place to better exercise your remarkable sales talents. This usually involves a career decision.

P.S.: CREATE OPPORTUNITIES

There's nothing wrong with selling to nonaffluent consumers. However, the fact that you're reading this book suggests you are already selling upmarket or considering an upmarket move. If your product line appeals mainly to nonaffluent consumers, you need to make a career change. Example: KIA makes good inexpensive cars that target nonaffluent consumers. Modeled after Japanese cars that took the middle class by storm, they don't afford an opportunity to move upmarket. Toyota and Nissan invested billions to create the Lexus and Infiniti brands in their effort to move upmarket. The Lexus sales experience is different from the Toyota sales experience. A salesperson with one company isn't better than the other; they're merely focused on different market segments.

Unlike automotive manufacturers, salespeople don't have to invest huge amounts of capital to move upmarket, but they *do* have to invest considerable time and energy to find opportunities to engage their affluent sales skills.

Once you've sold yourself on moving upmarket, your next challenge is admitting any fears associated with the sales process and then proceeding anyway.

Susan Jeffers wrote a wonderful little book, *Feel the Fear and Do It Anyway*. According to Dr. Jeffers, fear prevents most people from maximizing their potential. She's not referring to fear of death or dismemberment, but to psychological fears—the devilish voices of doubt that infect us with their sweet negatives.

Complete the following "worst fear" exercise. If possible, do it with a colleague.

WORST FEAR EXERCISE

In the space following, note a big affluent sales opportunity that makes you uncomfortable. Then jot down the worst possible outcome if you were to pursue it. Now that you've identified the worst case scenario, score yourself on the likelihood of it occurring. We find it helpful to obtain peer feedback on the exercise, so share this with a colleague. Discuss what you've written. Ideally, your colleague should complete the exercise with you so you can talk about your findings. Finally, write down a course of action that will help you overcome the mental hurdles.

• Affluent sales situation that makes you uncomfortable:

_____

_____

_____

_____

• Worst thing that could happen if you pursued it:

_____

_____

_____

_____

- Probability of worst case scenario occurring: (low) 1 2 3 4 5 6 7 8 9 10 (high): ____
- Peer feedback:

_____

_____

_____

_____

- Course of action planned:

_____

_____

_____

_____

We're always amazed by the peer-to-peer discussions that take place during the feedback session of this exercise. The two most common fears are fear of rejection and fear of embarrassment. When discussions move to the "worst thing that could possibly happen," they often take a hilarious turn: "I could break out in a full body sweat," "I might faint," "I might start babbling like an idiot," "I'll come across as stupid," "I'll appear desperate," and so on. It's a catharsis, all these affluent sales people discussing something they've kept hidden in their mental closets. The revelations produce lots of laughter and good feelings, especially feelings of relief.

The "Ah-ha!" moment of the discussion usually occurs when the probability of experiencing a worst-case scenario is assessed. Invariably, the odds are always remote, with the most extreme fears rated as having the lowest probability of occurring. Even the basic fear of rejection, which *is* more likely to occur, loses power when discussed with a peer. It becomes just another "part of the job."

What's interesting to observe is the course of action that's most often proposed. It's almost always "feel the fear and do it anyway."

Don't deny your fears. Recognize what's bothering you, and prepare for it. Know that rejection is part of the affluent sales game, but go for it anyway. The more masterful you become in the art of affluent sales, the less you'll encounter rejection and the mental hurdles that have held you back.

SUMMARY

Many sales professionals have gone upmarket by mastering the art of affluent sales. There's no better path to affluence for sales professionals than acquiring affluent clients. What's fascinating about professionals who have successfully gone upmarket is that many have continued striving for ever loftier heights, targeting the very wealthiest echelons.

Once you acquire the proper mind-set, searching for bigger and bigger opportunities becomes part of your DNA.

Research Facts

- Sixty percent of all consumer spending is done by households with annual incomes of $250,000 or more.
- For affluent consumers, the second biggest salesperson turnoff is lack of knowledge. The number one turnoff is salespeople who are too pushy.
- The net worth of the average affluent household is $3,624,118, compared with $185,750 for the average nonaffluent household.
- Annual affluent household spending is nearly six times that of nonaffluent households: $167,332 versus $28,039.

Taking Action

- Begin your search for upmarket opportunities.
- Commit to developing the mind-set of a master affluent salesperson.
- Determine where you will have to enhance your knowledge of products and services, as well as the competition.
- Assess your earning potential, and compare the earnings of top affluent sales professionals with the general population of salespeople.

Chapter 11   Overcoming Affluent Sales Reluctance

*The affluent are far more educated than the nonafflu-
ent: 55 percent have completed graduate school vs. 12
percent of the nonaffluent.*
> —Factoid, 2013 APD Research

You can overcome the fear of moving upmarket and still find yourself reluctant to proactively sell your services in affluent circles. In fact, when selling to the affluent, nothing impedes success more than affluent sales reluctance. It's the first cousin of fear, not as primal, but career hindering just the same. "I'm the mayor. I know everyone, and I rub shoulders with all the movers and shakers, but I feel awkward bringing up business with these people," said Jerry during a break at one of our Art of Selling to the Affluent workshops. "I don't want to come across as just another pushy salesperson. The mere thought of that makes me uncomfortable, but I know I'm leaving a lot of business on the table."

You'd think that campaigning for mayor, much less winning the election, would have purged Jerry's system of affluent sales reluctance, but it didn't.

What Jerry learned was that campaigning for votes and selling services to upscale consumers are two very different ventures. First, although few affluent voters trust politicians, they usually adopt the view that "somebody has to be mayor, so I may as well vote for the lesser of two evils." Second, most of the city's voters are nonaffluent. Finally, in Jerry's city, the mayor's job is an unpaid, part-time position.

From Jerry's psychological perspective, managing a political campaign had very little in common with selling professional services to the affluent. In fact, the campaign did almost nothing to cure Jerry of affluent sales reluctance. He's not alone. In Jerry's world (financial services), at least 90 percent of professionals suffer from this affliction.

Without meaning to add fuel to the fires of affluent call reluctance, there *are* valid causes for this debilitating mindset. Affluent consumers are less trusting, more skeptical, and more cynical than they were before the Great Recession—and they weren't an "easy sell" before then. The affluent can be a very intimidating bunch.

This is nothing new. Affluent sales reluctance has always been the "crazy uncle in the basement" that nobody wants to talk about. Salespeople are often afflicted with this career-damaging malady, but it's rare for them to admit it, much less work to overcome it. Instead, they complain about their company; talk about how difficult it's become to satisfy clients; take issue with the quality of the products/services they represent; and rationalize with some lame excuse like "Nobody's going to spend that much money for XYZ (product or services)."

You will rarely (i.e., virtually never) hear a salesperson confess to affluent sales reluctance unless you attend professional coaching or counseling sessions. There's a stigma attached to the problem, not unlike the stigma attached to athletes who "choke" under pressure. As a salesperson, confessing to affluent sales reluctance is like admitting that you're not made of the 'right stuff.' What kind of wimp is intimidated by his prospects? The sufferer must not have what it takes. She or he must be a mental weakling.

THOU SHALT OVERCOME

Affluent sales reluctance is a form of *social self-consciousness*, a topic to which I devoted an entire chapter of my first book. Because it presents a major speed bump to affluent sales success, I've decided to be more direct and refer to it here as *affluent sales reluctance*.

During my research for *The Art of Selling to the Affluent*, I interviewed George Dudley on the topic of social self-consciousness. Dudley and Shannon Goodson are co-authors of *The Psychology of Sales Call Reluctance: Earning What You're Worth*, in which they define social self-consciousness in salespeople as shunning "prospects of wealth, prestige, power, education or social standing."[1] Dudley explains the significance of social self-consciousness to this way:

---

[1] George Dudley and Shannon Goodson, *The Psychology of Sales Call Reluctance: Earning What You're Worth* (Dallas: Behavioral Sciences Research Press, 1999), 119.

One reason social self-consciousness is such a dangerous form of sales call reluctance is that it flies well under the radar of all but one sales selection test. That's because it is so highly "localized." Only one form of prospecting becomes impaired. All other forms are left unbothered. That means candidates may not be shy, timid, or even inexperienced. Their other prospecting skills may dazzle recruiters. Personality-based tests are notorious for failing to detect specific prospecting problems like social self-consciousness, and award them scores like "highly recommend." That illusion persists only until it's time to contact prospective buyers with wealth, education, power or social standing.[2]

During the interview, Dudley made it clear that social self-consciousness was *extremely* common. In fact, he implied that it could be found in nearly everyone. He also explained that no one is born with social self-consciousness. It's a learned behavior that is highly contagious. (The fact that it's contagious may explain why more than 90 percent of Jerry's colleagues are similarly challenged.) Even more important to note is that even people who have built successful careers selling to the nonaffluent may struggle with this affliction once they turn their attention to affluent consumers.

IS THIS A PROBLEM?

The following is a simple self-assessment that will help you take an honest look at your mindset vis-à-vis affluent sales. Since most salespeople experience affluent sales reluctance at some point in their careers, it's important to diagnose the symptoms as soon as possible. Although affluent sales reluctance is simple to overcome, few salespeople ever get past it because they don't spot the problem. Those who *do* overcome it out-earn their colleagues by a ratio of 10 to 1, or even more!

---

[2]Ibid., 125.

Are any of the following an issue for you?

1. I often feel that affluent clients and prospects make unreasonable demands or that they have unreasonable expectations.
2. I get the feeling that the affluent are talking down to me.
3. I can't be myself when working with the affluent. I'm always on guard.
4. I tend to become resentful when trying to meet the expectations of affluent clients.
5. I'm uncomfortable socializing in affluent spheres of influence.
6. I take rejections from affluent prospects more personally than those from nonaffluent prospects.
7. At times, I'm intimidated by the questions asked by affluent clients and prospects.
8. I'm not as comfortable communicating with the affluent as I am with nonaffluent consumers. I tend to let affluent sales opportunities pass.
9. I set affluent sales goals, but have not been able to achieve them.
10. I find myself engaging in nonproductive activities that prevent me from marketing my products/services to the affluent.

If seven or more items are an issue for you, you should take significant action. For three or more items, moderate action is needed. If none of these is an issue for you, no action is needed.

TAKING ACTION

An honest self-assessment is your first step in the preparation phase. Now it's time to review your sales activities over the past month.

Step 1. Preparation

- Can you identify affluent sales opportunities that you let pass you by? If so, how could you have handled the situation differently to facilitate the sale?

- Can you identify avoidance patterns that have kept you from selling your products/services to the affluent? If so, create a plan of action to help you break free from these habits. These patterns must be broken.

- Are you an expert in your product/service to the extent that you can answer virtually any question asked by an affluent client or prospect? If not, you need to expand the depth and breadth of your product and industry knowledge and/or identify experts in your firm or industry who can assist you.

- Can you articulate your value proposition with ease and clarity? If not, you must adopt your firm's value proposition and make it your own. This often requires simplifying and shortening the message.

- Can you visualize yourself articulating the value proposition to an affluent prospect and completing the sale?

- Determine which affluent prospects you can proactively contact. If this seems daunting, think of prospects with whom you've yet to conduct business or those, in your estimation, who would probably make good clients. Create a list, complete with a contact schedule.

- Identify which affluent clients you'll call for the purpose of requesting introductions to people in their spheres of influence— people who could become future clients.

- Develop a plan for socializing in affluent circles—not for business opportunities, but for affluent "acclimation."

- Create an ideal daily action plan.

Step 2. Mental Rehearsal

The best athletes in the world practice the art of visualization. Whether on the golf course, the baseball diamond, or the basketball court, elite athletes are famous for visualizing their performance in advance of the execution. They understand that the difference between winning and losing is usually mental. They also know that when they visualize success, they often increase the odds of achieving it.

Elite affluent sales professionals are no different. They see themselves as "one" with their affluent prospects, developing a rapport, answering questions, and sealing deals. Step 2 is about visualization. Visualize every aspect of your daily affluent sales routine. This can include:

- Communicating naturally and confidently with an affluent prospect.
- Answering questions with the conversational ease of a knowledgeable professional.
- Developing a rapport with an affluent prospect and getting her business.
- Calling an affluent client and asking to be introduced to someone in his affluent sphere of influence.
- Contacting a prospective affluent client and setting up a meeting.
- Socializing in affluent circles (for nonbusiness purposes).
- Viewing yourself as an affluent person.

Step 3. Power Pose

Research conducted at Harvard Business School and the Haas School of Business at the University of California, Berkeley, now provides us with evidence that our posture—how we pose—can literally change a person's hormones. This in turn, impacts behavior.

The research referred to a study in which job applicants who engaged in a few minutes of power posing prior to a mock job interview created a much better first impression and were deemed "more likely to be chosen for hire." Power posing: standing with good posture with hands on hips, standing with arms raised overhead like you won a race, standing at your desk with hands on desk leaning forward, sitting with your hands clasped behind your head, sitting and leaning back with feet on desk and hands clasped behind head can all help you build confidence prior to a meeting. Using these poses in an actual meeting is rarely appropriate.

Spend a few minutes engaged in a power pose *before* interacting with an affluent client or prospect.

Step 4. Action

Regardless of how you feel (remember—feel the fear and do it anyway), take the actions you identified in Step 1. The idea is to *feel* the fear and anxiety, and take action in spite of those feelings. Whether it's asking for the order, calling a prospect to schedule a meeting, or answering questions, strategic action is the key to affluent sales success. Strategic action is the cure (yes, cure!) for affluent sales reluctance.

- Prioritize your preparations in Step 1 and take appropriate actions, with the top-priority item implemented first.
- Perform your version of a mental rehearsal of the upcoming day. Visualize yourself executing all of your prepared and prioritized action steps exactly as you would like them to occur.
- Follow through on your ideal sales day as visualized (determined in Step 1).
- At the end of each day, outline your upcoming ideal sales day.
- Once a week, interact socially (for nonbusiness reasons) in affluent circles.

To overcome affluent call reluctance, pride must take a back seat. Few salespeople like to admit they're self-conscious around affluent clients and prospects. No one likes to admit that he or she is intimidated by another person, especially when there seems to be no valid reason for it. However, if the affliction goes untreated, affluent call reluctance will develop, and that's something no affluent salesperson can live with. Hence, it's important to take corrective measures.

CONTROLLING THE DEVILISH VOICE OF DOUBT

There is profound truth in this famous saying of the Buddha:

> We are what we think.
> All that we are arises with our thoughts.
> With our thoughts we make the world. . . .

What Buddhists have long known, and what salespeople need to know, is that thoughts shape the personal reality in which we live. However, thoughts don't constitute objective reality unless you allow them to dominate your mind. For example, have you ever gotten angry because a boss or a colleague failed to return your calls or emails right away? In response, did you then conduct imaginary conversations in your head with the person, chastising him for ignoring your messages? Maybe an argument ensued (in your head) in which you yelled at the person. If the person was your boss, you may have even imagined quitting your job in a fit of pique. But then, did you receive a response from your boss or colleague, at which point you learned he was on vacation or handling a family crisis? Didn't you feel foolish for having had these emotional outbursts in your mind?

This type of scenario points to the roots of social self-consciousness and affluent sales reluctance. We humans usually allow our minds to race around in uncontrolled fashions. In this undisciplined state, our thoughts generate strong emotions and expectations that have no basis in objective reality, but they can *seem* as real as the most concrete objects. If we expect to be nervous, tongue-tied, and embarrassed in the presence of people that we consider our social or intellectual betters, we may create a "thoughtscape" in which anxiety leads to disaster. We may then replay these hypothetical scenarios in our minds again and again until they form our expectation of what *will* happen.

However, if we banish negative thoughts and expectations with positive thoughts and expectations, we're more likely to create a reality in which success occurs naturally and fluidly—almost effortlessly. (Zen Masters refer to this as "effortless effort.")

As a practitioner of Zen meditation, Tiger Woods puts this approach into practice every time he steps onto the golf course. He has learned not to become attached to future outcomes. He has learned not to obsess over a yet-to-happen performance. Instead of worrying about what could go wrong, he trusts his ability to perform the actions necessary to guide the ball to its destination. Time and again, his focus is on *doing*—not thinking.

This may seem like New Age mumbo jumbo, but it's based in psychological fact. Because our thoughts have such a profound influence on our behavior, it's critical to imbue ourselves with confidence, calm, and a laser-like focus on what we plan to *do*—not on events beyond our control. We have to let go of *what if* and focus on what we're *doing* in the moment.

I refer to these *what if* thoughts as the "devilish voice of doubt." If we listen to this voice, we will never achieve our goals. The human mind is hardwired to accept those devilish thoughts ("they're not going to do business with me") as truth because it can't distinguish objective facts from perceived facts. If we truly *believe* something is real, it may as well *be* real.

Programming your mind for affluent sales success is essential for mastering affluent selling. Since our *thinking* programs our mind, everything you are today is the result of your thinking up to this point. Everything you become will be the result of your thoughts from this point forward.

Controlling that devilish voice of doubt, that internal saboteur, requires a technique I call *conscious thought management*. There are four steps to a conscious thought management action plan. The first three are easy to implement. They can and should be done each day. The fourth will take more preparation, but afterward, it's also very easy to implement.

Technique 1: Starting Out Right

When you awaken in the morning, your subconscious mind is more amenable to new programming than at any other time. As soon as you wake, say to yourself: "I feel terrific! I feel great!" Then spend 20 to 30 minutes reading something inspirational, motivational, or instructional. Do *not* listen to the news or anything that might stimulate negative thinking. We are all energy forces, so make sure your energy is not only positive but positively infectious.

Technique 2: Getting Back on Track

We all have down times during the day—coffee breaks, meal breaks, or times of travel between sales calls. Those are the times we are most susceptible to that devilish voice of doubt, especially if we just experienced a problem with a client, or we find ourselves getting involved with minutia to avoid interacting with affluent prospects.

Ah, but what do you do?

First, be honest with yourself. Recognize that you're off track. Next, do something totally unrelated to affluent selling. Walk outside and enjoy the fresh air for five minutes. Take a walk around the block. Get a cup of coffee. There are endless things you can do to get back in the mental game. Finally, get into the habit of filling down time by listening to inspirational messages or reading. Fill your conscious mind with positive thoughts.

Technique 3: Associating with the Right People

Attitudes are contagious. Fear breeds fear. Laziness fosters laziness. Goal-focused activity breeds goal-focused activity. What's more, the people we associate with often have the greatest influence on us.

If you're serious about mastering the art of affluent sales, which is the salesperson's fast track to personal affluence, associate with successful people. These are the people who will support your efforts, offer constructive advice, and serve as role models. Granted, there aren't a lot of successful role models floating around, which means you'll have to go out of your way to rub shoulders with these positive high achievers with can-do spirits (the world of the affluent).

Today's affluent, much like affluent of days past, cluster together. Like the saying "birds of a feather flock together," it's important to join a flock of the high-achieving affluent to which you'll sell products and services. Ironically, many of the high achievers who will champion your efforts will become loyal affluent clients themselves.

Note: Prepare for the envy of peers who aren't willing to pay the price. Every salesperson would love to master affluent sales and become affluent, but few are willing to pay the price. Consequently, they become jealous of anyone who is actively mastering the craft. This usually takes the form of subtle sabotage, including well-timed comments such as: "Why are you bending over backward for that client?" "Do you really think that prospect is going to do business with you?" "Our offering isn't as good as they're telling us." And so on.

Be ready and able to detect a jealous saboteur quickly and then avoid that person. Whether this requires avoiding a new associate or adding someone new to your reference group, make your associations a conscious choice, and be sure to choose carefully.

Technique 4: Creating a Self-Affirmation Recording

We've been teaching this technique to salespeople for over 30 years. The fact is, garbage into the mind produces garbage in the form of behavior. The secret to success is developing a system to replace any "input garbage" with self-affirmation.

Develop the habit of using daily self-affirmations. Initially, this will require you to write a series of affirmations and then record them on your MP3 player or i-Phone so you can listen to them daily. I know this seems over the top, but playing the affirmation will be worth the effort. Creating a self-affirmation recording is simple. It's based on the 7-7-7 rule:

- Seven affirmation statements.
- Repeated seven times each.
- Spaced seven seconds apart.

In our experience, the greatest impact is achieved by looking at your total life and then seeking to create balance via the seven affirmation statements. To achieve this balance, focus on areas that you *want to change* and also areas that you *don't want to neglect*.

I recommend that clients segment their affirmations into two groups. Develop four statements for affluent sales—affirmations that target specific areas related to affluent sales success. Then develop three statements that focus on any combination of the following: physical health, mental health, spiritual well-being, and marriage, family, social, educational, or personal growth. The words you select for the affirmation statements are important. They will determine the pictures that form in your subconscious, so follow these guidelines:

- *Personal:* Open each statement with words such as I am, I have, It's easy for me to, I enjoy, I love. . . . Do not say "My wife will praise me when I make a big sale to an affluent client." Instead, say "I love selling my [services/products] to the affluent."

- *Positive:* Focus on what you ideally want to see in the future. Leave your problems behind. Do not say "I am no longer going to be fat." Instead, say "I am healthy, fit, and enjoy being at my natural weight."

- *Present tense:* Phrase your affirmations as if they were true right now. This will prompt your subconscious mind to automatically treat the affirmation as *reality*. Do not say "I will master the art of affluent sales." Instead, say "I am master of affluent sales."

- *Comparison free:* Comparing yourself with others creates a false sense of reality in your mind. Commit to acquiring the qualities of the high achievers you admire, but do not compare yourself with them. Do not say "I am going to earn more commissions than Mary." Instead, say "I am earning $250,000 a year [you select the dollar amount]."

- *Private:* Affirmations are for private use. Don't share them with anyone except a working partner who's using the same technique. People who don't use conscious thought management rarely understand the process, and some may try to sabotage your efforts (while claiming they're just trying to help). By keeping affirmation statements to yourself, you'll be able to say what you really want to say.

We've found these next three steps to be most effective in helping clients write their seven affirmation statements:

1. Think of a dimension of your life that you want to change. Write that *change area* on a piece of paper.
2. Imagine yourself in a situation in which you've already made that change and are enjoying the results. Describe that *image* next.
3. Use whatever you imagined to guide you in writing a powerful *affirmation statement* (as outlined above).

MAKING MIND-SET CHANGES USING AFFIRMATIONS

Change area: I would like to be confident socializing with the affluent.

Image: I am introduced to the affluent neighbor of a client. I am relaxed and full of positive energy, and I easily develop a rapport. My eye contact is warm and friendly; my handshake is firm and engaging. My abilities to ask questions and listen allow me to "reverse uncover" a potential need for my professional services.

Affirmation statement: I develop rapport naturally with affluent prospects.

The following are samples of affluent affirmations that other salespeople have successfully used to overcome social self-consciousness:

- I love socializing in affluent circles.
- I'm relaxed and confident when talking to affluent clients and prospects.
- I love serving my affluent clients.
- I naturally develop rapport with people of affluence.
- I love prospecting socially in affluent circles.
- My antenna is always out for affluent opportunities.
- My affluent selling skills are seamless.

- I love working with the affluent.
- I'm skilled at asking questions and listening.
- I ask for personal introductions and referrals at every opportunity.
- I am totally focused on activities that enhance my affluent sales.

An effective method for developing and benefiting from affirmations is placing each one on a 3-by-5-inch card. Carry those cards with you everywhere you go, and refer to them whenever you feel the need—or even when you don't feel the need (knowing the kind of extra energy that reviewing your affirmations can provide).

As George Dudley told me in the interview conducted for my first book on affluent sales, "When diagnosed early, social self-consciousness is easy to correct." If you are saying, "I enjoy meeting with affluent prospects" seven times each day, you are talking the right talk. You also need to walk the walk so that your affirmation is consistent with your action. It's all about consistently doing the right things, the right way, to the right affluent people, for the right reasons."

SUMMARY

Today's affluent want to be served on a personal level. Therefore, today's salespeople must *stop* avoidance habits (busy work) that prevent them from personally interacting with affluent clients and prospects. According to George Dudley and Shannon Goodson, avoidance patterns are caused by social self-consciousness. They must be overcome, or a salesperson runs the risk of developing affluent call reluctance.

No one is born with social self-consciousness. It is learned and highly contagious, but so is affluent sales success. The idea is to master conscious thought management, feel the fear, and go for the business anyway. Engaging in affluent sales activities and socializing in affluent circles, combined with the subconscious programming tactics outlined in this chapter, will cure most salespeople of social self-consciousness. When it is accurately identified and the proper remedy is provided, affluent sales reluctance is relatively easy to correct.

Whenever you find yourself setting affluent sales targets and failing to follow through, it's likely you're being held back by affluent sales reluctance. Another clue is if you avoid socializing in affluent circles because you feel uncomfortable around people of wealth.

Your first step is to be totally honest with yourself on this issue. The next step is to take appropriate actions to overcome any social self-consciousness that may be blocking your road to success. These actions occur in three phases: preparation, mental rehearsal, and action.

Research Facts

- Thirty-five percent of all salespeople struggle with social self-consciousness.
- Social self-consciousness has been documented in more than 73 industries.

Taking Action

- Take the social self-consciousness self-assessment in this chapter. Note that this will only benefit you if you are totally honest with yourself.
- Practice the mental rehearsal step so you can begin using it immediately with each face-to-face encounter with the affluent in your community.
- Review the four techniques relating to the action steps in this chapter. Select and begin implementing those you feel will help you the most. Do not overlook "Technique 4: Creating a Self-Affirmation Recording." It will take time to create these affirmations, but the technique often helps more than any of the other three.
- Practice your power poses.
- Go among the affluent several times a week. Using the mental rehearsal step and action step techniques to reinforce those efforts, you will be surprised how quickly any social self-consciousness you have will become a thing of the past.

Chapter 12 Maximizing Your Affluent Sales Opportunities

Affluent consumers are the largest single group that works up to 70 hours per week.
—Factoid, 2013 APD Research

Here is where we put everything together. Are you ready to tackle the psychological risks (few affluent salespeople encounter physical risks) and invest the necessary time and energy for success?

It's been my experience that hard work is not the biggest challenge to mastering the art of affluent sales. Most salespeople are hard workers. However, working hard and working smart don't always go hand-in-hand. A good salesperson who doesn't apply those skills to selling in the affluent market is on a fool's errand. Sorry, but that's my opinion. And to those salespeople who are already working in the affluent world, but aren't making the effort to improve their skills, shame on you. You won't walk very far down the path to affluence and professional fulfillment.

To obtain the maximum value from this chapter, use it to either renew your vow of achieving personal affluence or to make the initial commitment. You'll be venturing outside your comfort zone on this journey. Without a strong commitment, you'll be tempted to retreat into your comfort zone. This temptation has derailed many a good salesperson.

Our affluent sales coaches understand this only too well. They know that activity drives the dream of personal affluence, so they make certain that "students" perform the necessary activities, regardless of their comfort level.

In the spirit of action, I recommend that you make this book your affluent tool kit. Write notes in the columns, underline passages for use as quick-glance reminders, and keep the book handy for easy reference. At this stage, you probably know which areas you must address to maximize affluent sales opportunities. The challenge now is what you should do with that knowledge.

Create your own crystal ball. Look within yourself and imagine what *could* be if you applied the ideas, strategies, and tactics in this book. This is known as *envisioning your future*.

My wife's experience with a new car illustrates the value of this technique.

Sandy recently encountered a problem with her new Mercedes. After driving this "crossover" vehicle for two weeks, she complained that it was too big. "I don't feel comfortable in parking lots or pulling into the garage." I thought she simply needed time to adjust to the vehicle's size, since she'd always driven Mercedes station wagons in the past.

One year later, Sandy visited the dealership because of an issue with the battery. (*Note:* During this time, nobody from the dealership followed up regarding her satisfaction with the car, and Sandy did not ask to see her original salesman when she visited the dealership.) While chatting with a service assistant about her preference for station wagons, the service assistant mentioned that there might be a station wagon on the lot, so she buzzed a salesman. However, the salesman told Sandy that he'd sold the station wagon the previous afternoon.

Disappointed, Sandy requested an estimate of her car's trade-in value and instructed the salesman to call her the next time a station wagon (new or slightly used) arrived on the lot. At the time of this writing it's nearly six months later and she hasn't heard from the salesman. A couple of weeks ago, I drove past this dealership. What did I see, parked amid the SUVs and crossovers? A station wagon!

I think this luxury automobile maker would benefit from training their sales force on the dos and don'ts of affluent sales. No amount of "bells and whistles" can compensate for the lack of personal attention my wife received from the sales staff at this dealership.

Can you imagine Sandy's response if the original salesman had sent her a bouquet of flowers or a bottle of wine on her birthday? While visiting the dealership for service on her battery, she would definitely have asked to see him. There would be *no* chance that she'd consider another brand of automobile.

What a shame that neither salesperson had the "eye of the tiger"—that neither made a commitment to affluent salesmanship.

Following up with an interested prospect should be standard operating procedure among even mediocre salespeople.

CAN YOU ENVISION YOUR AFFLUENT FUTURE?

If you don't dream, you're merely going through the motions. If, like the Mercedes reps who dealt with Sandy, you don't project yourself into the future, your sales history will become the harbinger of your sales future.

To *envision* is to imagine something that doesn't yet exist, and it answers two questions:

1. What am I capable of becoming?
2. What quality of business and personal life do I want two or three years from now?

Robert Louis Stevenson said, "To be what we are, and to become what we are capable of becoming, is the only end in life." If 12 months from now you haven't embarked on your affluent sales journey, it's unlikely that your business and personal life have changed or are about to change.

My objective in writing this sequel to *The Art of Selling to the Affluent* is to update the pathways to affluent sales success. Although much has changed as a result of the Great Recession, much remains the same. What's changed is that I'm encountering more and more salespeople who have allowed the recession to force them off track. They went from positivity and passion to a "glass half empty" mindset. Recognizing that you need to overcome this attitude is not enough. Knowing what to do is not enough. You must know which daily activities to pursue. That's why it's critical to envision your future, which is best accomplished by:

1. *Contrasting* where you are today with where you want to be in 12 months, so the gap between *now* and *want to be* will become clear.

2. *Avoiding worry* over how you will close the gap between now and 12 months from now. Be confident that you will achieve your future by envisioning it.

Selecting what to contrast is important. Every item should be measurable, so you can identify how far you've come and how far you still need to go. Each gap you spot becomes a "work in progress." The most obvious items to contrast are:

- Average monthly commissions
- Number of *new* affluent clients
- Number of *qualified* affluent prospects
- Average monthly income

Think about how these four items are interrelated. Be honest about the numbers associated with each of these areas *today*. This is especially true when it comes to assessing qualified prospects. When conducting this exercise, many salespeople inflate their pipelines of prospects. Suddenly, anyone they've ever met is a potential client. Don't fall into that trap. Your pipeline is the biggest indicator of future affluent sales. Make sure you're accurate regarding prospects' levels of affluence *and* interest levels.

Select challenging, but realistic, numbers regarding the commissions, sales, and income you want to achieve over the next 12 months. With those numbers in place, select measurable activities linked to those goals. For instance, if your goal was to lose 30 pounds, you would want to count your daily exercise and calorie intake. In the sales world, an example might be :

- Average weekly introductions and referrals to affluent prospects
- Average number of affluent prospects you are actively pursuing
- Memberships in "one-with-the-affluent" organizations
- Number and types of activities and events you will attend to place yourself in the path of the affluent people you want to attract
- Number of affluent names and email addresses in your database

- Number of affluent social media connections: LinkedIn, Facebook, Twitter, and so on
- Average number of digital promotions sent each month: via email, text, and social media

Here is where elite affluent sales professionals get creative. They understand that it's impossible for me to include all the items pertaining to their personal situations in this book. Therefore, they are careful to select items that are measurable and directly linked to achieving more affluent sales.

Each item must take you, step-by-step, item-by-item, where you want to be 12 months from now. There is rarely one monumental event that can maximize your affluent sales potential. Instead, every item represents part of a disciplined step-by-step process, with each new step building on the previous one.

After you've established your affluent sales goals and identified gaps that must be closed, your next step is to determine the actions you will take to close the gaps.

CLOSING THE GAPS

The activities in which you're currently engaged (effective or not) are done out of habit. Experts tell us that 80 percent of what we think and do is "habit driven." Habits are formed over time and stored in our subconscious. They eliminate the need to carefully consider every action in our lives.

Mental habits are behavioral patterns that shape our attitudes and actions. Over time, what we repeatedly think and do from habit becomes comfortable, creating a *comfort zone*. The extent to which you can break free of your comfort zone and use new knowledge to shape new attitudes and behavioral patterns will determine the answer to the "How will this new knowledge change my daily activity?" question. What's most important is the behavioral pattern that will emerge from this. Will it be an *avoidance pattern* or an *achievement pattern*?

I'm going to make an obvious assumption: You would like to apply what you've learned in this book to increase your affluent sales and make your envisioned future a reality. Given this assumption, which of the following behavioral patterns best describes how you will do that?

- You review the sections of this book that are important to you. As you study, you make notes about how you will implement the *how-to* information. You focus that preparation on tasks such as researching the events you might plan to show appreciation for your clients and expand your network, how you will create a better first impression in both personal appearance and in your sales environment, the steps you need to take to overcome any lingering affluent call reluctance, setting up your sphere-of-influence model for each affluent client, brainstorming about stimulating affluent buzz, and so forth. As you read and write, you are aware that feelings of doubt arise now and then. At these points, you stop for a while and do something else until the feelings fade.
- You commit to accomplishing three action items by the end of next week:
  1. Initiate a face-to-face contact with one affluent prospect a day.
  2. Surprise and delight two affluent clients.
  3. Ask one affluent client for a personal introduction to someone in their sphere of influence.
- You write down the specific steps required to achieve each action item by next Friday. Afterward, you schedule these steps as fixed daily activities (FDAs) in a day planner.
- Or you begin working on those activities immediately, determined to complete at least three before the end of the day.

Which of these scenarios represents an *avoidance pattern* and which represents *achievement pattern*? Most important, which best describes your natural tendencies? Are you a doer? Or, are you going to think about it, prepare some more, and "get ready" to apply what you've learned from this book? Please don't fall into the latter category. "Getting ready to get ready" is a vicious cycle that will derail the best of intentions. Mastering the fine art of affluent sales requires action.

ACTIVATING YOUR ACHIEVEMENT CYCLE

All of us have a devilish voice of doubt, which often surfaces when we commit to ambitious goals. I agreed to an ambitious deadline to write this book, since I'd already completed the research and written a handful of white papers on the topic. Every so often, however, the nagging voice invaded my mind: "Am I going to make this deadline?" I quieted the voice by adhering to my disciplined writing schedule—by *doing the required activities.*

Are you still thinking "Affluent selling is too overwhelming" or "I don't think I could ever double my income or I have nothing to offer that's really special"?

If so, you're in good company. The doubt sequence usually begins in earnest after you've made a heartfelt commitment to your goals. That process by itself usually pulls people out of their comfort zone. And then they begin thinking about what it will take to close all of those gaps to achieve their goals.

It's important to understand that everyone encounters this sort of doubt, but it doesn't have to knock you off track. The secret is recognizing doubt when it occurs, and knowing that your new course of action will keep you on track and quiet the doubts. Recognize how the adage "garbage in, garbage out" applies to your thinking. Recognize how your thoughts (the devilish voice = garbage) directly affect your behavior.

Twenty-five years ago, Dr. Shad Helmstetter wrote *The Self-Talk Solution,* which I still recommend today. Dr. Helmstetter wrote, "One of the most important discoveries in recent years has been the role our own casual thinking plays in shaping of our lives."[1] Neuroscientists have discovered that thoughts are electrical impulses that trigger both electrical and chemical reactions in the brain. The impact is significant, whether the thoughts are good or bad. Negative thinking doesn't simply result in continued negative thinking. It also stimulates negative behavior, and that's when things get serious.

What we do is driven by three components: feeling, thinking, and doing. When we allow negative feelings to emerge from our subconscious and shape our thinking, this produces the "I-can't-do-it" mind-set. We search for excuses to not do what we know we should do. We allow negative feelings to produce negative thinking that produces inactivity, which allows us to stay inside our comfort zone.

Activating your achievement cycle can reverse this process because it changes the sequence from feeling-thinking-doing to doing-thinking-feeling.

Doing is goal-driven, and doing is almost completely under your control. That's how you break out of your comfort zone—by *doing* activities linked to a goal. Keep your goals in front of you and *do* what you have to do. Once your goals are set and the gap you must close becomes clear, you're ready to activate your achievement cycle.

ACHIEVEMENTS OF THE PAST

This is one of my favorite exercises. I've guided thousands of salespeople through it, and it never ceases to amaze me how quickly it produces "Ah-ha!" moments. It's interesting to observe how instinctive the achievement cycle is to human beings. The fact is, everyone has activated this cycle at some point in the past. In my experience, the difference between salespeople who never reach their full potential and elite performers is that elite salespeople consistently activate their achievement cycles, whereas

---

[1] Shad Helmstetter, *The Self-Talk Solution* (New York: Pocket Books, 1988), 14.

average performers engage in negative self-talk that sabotages their achievement cycles.

Revisit a major goal you set for yourself and think of how you achieved it. Chances are, this achievement didn't make you rich or famous, but I'll guarantee that it followed a predictable pattern. Reactivating this pattern will lead you to affluence.

Can you recall the goal? I'll bet it sends chills down your spine just thinking about it. I'd also wager that, as you remember the accomplishment, you'll recall being pulled far outside your comfort zone to achieve it.

I remember setting the goal of writing my first book. It was a completely new experience for me. Were all of my thoughts positive ones? Nope. The devilish voice of doubt poured poison in my ear on more than one occasion. Sitting in my den with a legal pad in my lap, I outlined the chapters of the book. There was complete quiet: no television, no music; just me sitting in a chair under a reading lamp with pen and paper. Sandy walked by, looked into the room, sensed something out of the ordinary and asked, "What are you doing?"

"I'm writing a book."

She entered the den and said, "You're writing a book?! You don't know how to write. And furthermore, who's ever going to read it?" She walked out of the room.

This memory might make Sandy seem unsupportive, but that's far from the truth. The fact is, she'd seen me waste time on various half-baked schemes many times before. She had no way of knowing that this was different. I had committed my heart and soul to writing the book. This was connected to my profession. At the same time, her comments echoed those of the devilish little voice, which was already saying, "Who's going to want to read anything you write?" At these times, I felt like a fraud—a pretender hoping he'd never be unmasked.

But again, my commitment to this goal was total. It was imprinted in my mind. Even though the devilish voice tried to sabotage my efforts, I proceeded to write. I forged ahead for the next 18 months, after which I became the proud author of my first published book.

Achieving this goal didn't make me famous or rich, but it validated the power of the achievement cycle—the cycle you are revisiting by recalling your past accomplishments. The secret is realizing that this cycle can be—and must be—reactivated over and over. Let's observe how it works in the context of your affluent sales goals.

Goal Commitment: Subconscious Imprinting

- *Envision your future* following the process outlined earlier in this chapter.
- *Repeat your goals* at the start of each week—or daily, if necessary. Write them down and speak them aloud over and over. Even if you've memorized them, read them at the beginning of each week. Refine them if you feel the need.
- *Visualize your goals* by sitting back, relaxing, and seeing yourself completing the steps required to achieve each goal. Notice how great you feel as a result, and you will begin to block the negative feelings that seem to emerge from nowhere.

Goal-Focused Action Steps

- *Define the fixed daily activities* you must perform to achieve your ambitious goals. You may not have to perform each activity every day, but you must perform the activities connected to your goals every day. That's why we call them fixed daily activities—to emphasize the importance of performing these goal-achieving activities every day.
- *Plan, schedule, perform, and measure weekly.* This has always been the formula for goal-based action: Plan your week and work your plan. The idea is to *plan* at the beginning of the week, Sunday afternoon, which activities (FDAs) you will do each day. You can *schedule* these activities on whatever calendar system you're using (we're currently using Outlook Express, which I have on my iPhone, iPad, and MacBook Air). *Perform* the FDAs scheduled for each day, noting how good it feels to cross each

activity off your calendar as it's completed. Then *measure* what you accomplished at the end of the week, noting how you are being systematically pulled toward your goals, which in turn helps you plan for the following week. It's an ongoing process.

For some people, executing the first planned activity can be the toughest step. I used to think that's because people usually schedule the activity that's most uncomfortable to get it over with. In other cases, people choose a first activity that isn't uncomfortable, but it triggers other, less comfortable activities. For example, one sales professional schedules a 15-minute meeting with his assistant every morning, and that meeting triggers every other high-impact affluent sales activity. He said, "Whenever I miss this meeting, which happens—not often, but it happens—I don't have a productive day."

Whether the first activity serves as a trigger or it is uncomfortable, one activity completed usually leads to another and another. Activity to activity, day by day, week after week, you will find yourself turning this goal-focused process into a habit. Some activities will get easier; others will continue pulling you outside your comfort zone. That's to be expected. There are three reasons for this, each beginning with a C:

1. *Conviction* is belief without proof. That's what you must do from the very outset. You must convince yourself that goals are achievable. You must be convinced that if you do the hard work, venture outside your comfort zone, and perform your FDAs, you will achieve the goals. When conviction is lacking, I see lots of finger pointing at company policies, poor management, down markets, and anything else that provides an excuse for inactivity. Look at the future you have envisioned. Set aside excuses, and believe without proof. As you take this step and each subsequent step, your confidence will grow.

2. *Confidence* is either the pillar or the killer of success. Confident people don't sit around thinking and talking. They get up and

go *do* it. Too much thinking can create the avoidance pattern described above. The most effective way to build confidence is by performing FDAs directly linked to a serious goal. You then become:

○ Convinced that your goals are the right ones.
○ Confident about taking the next step toward the goals.
○ Confident that you have the expertise to take the next step.
○ Confident that taking the next step will not only advance you toward the goals, but also enable you to gain the additional expertise and confidence for the next step. As confidence grows, competency grows along with it.

3. *Competence* evolves from experience, not from classes or books. Knowledge produces competence only when you use it to make mistakes, adjust, and find better ways to accomplish something. That's why face-to-face encounters with the affluent are so critical. They create experiences that enable you to learn, gain confidence, and become more competent. Competency is also the product of doing the right things, and experience is the only true test of what those right things are.

The key to success is performing the activities linked to your goals, even when that devilish little voice whispers "You can't pull this off." It means doing your FDAs even when you don't feel like it. Anyone can do what they want when they feel like doing it. If that was all it took to achieve a goal, everyone would be a success.

Once you are convinced you have the right goals and are actively pursuing them, your confidence will grow, your competence will improve, you will become one with your affluent clientele, and soon you, too, will be affluent. There is no other way.

STAYING ON YOUR CRITICAL PATH

I love the concept of the *critical path*. I've written about it many times and we coach to it. It was even the subtitle of one of my earlier books on selling. Some of you might recall that the concept grew out of a project planning and management technique that became popular in the 1960s. The goal is to focus on a handful of critical activities that must be done each day—activities so vital that failure to perform them will significantly delay your progress or even lead to failure. This path establishes boundaries for your activities and serves as an activity filter.

As a sales person, you could engage in many activities on a given day. Compare the *avoidance pattern* activities with the *achievement pattern* activities at the beginning of this chapter, and you will see what I mean. What you need to focus on is critical path activities—those described in the second scenario, not the first.

The critical path can also serve as an activity accelerator. The Critical Path Organizer on (Figure 12.1) will facilitate this process. When using the organizer, follow these guidelines:

- *Plan your week*. There are seven categories of face-to-face contacts (page 208). Your goal is to make a certain number of contacts each day. In the spaces provided, enter the names of the people you hope to contact followed by the contact code (see the bottom of the page).
  - Second, complete the Prospect Tracking section (page 211). This lets you review not just the number of prospects in the pipeline but their potential, as well as your strategy for transforming these prospects into customers.
  - Next, determine the number of contacts you'll make in each category, and record those numbers on your Weekly Prospecting Scorecard (see bottom of page 211).
  - Finally, make a list of Affluent Client Activities, Affluent Prospecting Activities, and Family and Health Activities in your Weekly Activity Scheduler (page 209).
- *Plan each day*. Enter the contacts and activities for that day in your Weekly Activity Scheduler (page 209). Then, add all your other time-driven FDAs for that day. You should meet with your support staff first thing in the morning to

Critical Path ORGANIZER   Week of ___/___/___ to ___/___/___

Face-to-Face Contacts

Activity Drives The Dream!   Type of Contact   Type of Contact

Client Retention Contacts		Objective: Strengthen Loyalty	

Client Upgrade Contacts		Objective: Introduce New Products or Services	

Strategic Networking (Civic/Social Involvement)		Objective: Get in Front of Affluent Opportunities	

Wow: Surprise and Delight / Intimate Events		Objective: Stimulate Affluent Buzz	

Affluent Prospect Introductions		Objective: Word of Mouth Influence	

Affluent Prospect Referrals		Objective: Bring into My Pipeline	

Affluent Prospect – Placing Myself in their Path		Objective: Bring into My Pipeline	

Type of Contact: P = Phone Call   E = Email   M = Scheduled Meeting   S = Social Event

Your Critical Path to Affluent Selling Success

FIGURE 12.1   The Critical Path Organizer

Weekly Activity SCHEDULER

Monday _____	Tuesday _____	Wednesday _____	Thursday _____
7 _____	7 _____	7 _____	7 _____
8 _____	8 _____	8 _____	8 _____
9 _____	9 _____	9 _____	9 _____
10 _____	10 _____	10 _____	10 _____
11 _____	11 _____	11 _____	11 _____
12 _____	12 _____	12 _____	12 _____
1 _____	1 _____	1 _____	1 _____
2 _____	2 _____	2 _____	2 _____
3 _____	3 _____	3 _____	3 _____
4 _____	4 _____	4 _____	4 _____
5 _____	5 _____	5 _____	5 _____
6 _____	6 _____	6 _____	6 _____
7 _____	7 _____	7 _____	7 _____
8 _____	8 _____	8 _____	8 _____
9 _____	9 _____	9 _____	9 _____
Phone/email/meeting: ✓	Phone/email/meeting: ✓	Phone/email/meeting: ✓	Phone/email/meeting: ✓

FIGURE 12.1   (continued)

		Other Activities TO SCHEDULE
Friday _____	**Saturday** _____	*Affluent Client* Activities
7 _____		
8 _____		
9 _____		
10 _____		
11 _____		
12 _____		
1 _____		*Affluent Prospecting* Activities
2 _____		
3 _____		
4 _____	**Sunday** _____	
5 _____		
6 _____		
7 _____		
8 _____		
9 _____		*Family and Health* Activities
Phone/email/meeting:	Phone/email/meeting:	

FIGURE 12.1 (continued)

Pipeline TRACKING

Name	Status[1]	Potential[2]	Strategy[3]
1			
2			
3			
4			
5			
6			
7			
8			
9			
10			
11			
12			
13			
14			
15			
16			
17			
18			

[1] C = Current N= New this Week	[2] Brief description of their interest in what you offer.	[3] Next steps to take with this potential client.

Weekly Metrics SCORECARD

Transfer from the previous pages.

CLIENT Contacts	Target	Actual
• Retention Contacts	_____	_____
• Upgrade Contacts	_____	_____
• Strategic Networking Contacts	_____	_____
• WOW Contacts	_____	_____

Affluent General Contacts	Target	Actual
• Civic Events	_____	_____
• Social Events	_____	_____

PROSPECT Contacts	Target	Actual
• Affluent Prospect—Introductions	_____	_____
• Affluent Prospect—Referral Contacts	_____	_____
• Affluent Prospect Contacts—From Placing Myself	_____	_____

FIGURE 12.1 (continued)

review the previous day and preview the FDAs for the day. Ask whether there is anything they need, and then provide whatever they need. This is the best way to segue from reactive to proactive.

- *Measure your weekly activity.* At the end of each week, record in your Weekly Prospecting Scorecard the actual number of contacts you made in each of the seven categories.
- *Analyze your weekly activity.* First, review the target versus actual numbers under your Weekly Prospecting Scorecard.
  - Where and why were you under target or over target?
  - What progress have you made with each of your prospects?
  - How effectively did you perform with each contact?
  - What changes do you want to make next week to improve performance?

The discipline that the Critical Path Organizer brings to your business development efforts far outweighs the time required to plan, record, and analyze the information. If you would like a copy, please email us at info@affluentsalestraining.com.

Now it's time to model the four key traits of top affluent sales professionals that we uncovered in our research. They're traits you're likely to find in top performers regardless of profession and they're likely to define your affluent sales career.

FOUR KEY TRAITS OF TOP AFFLUENT SALES PROFESSIONALS

Those who can master the art of affluent sales can make the transition to upmarket sales. In many circles, they are referred to as the "elite." My firm has studied these top performers for more than a decade and, though they hail from different disciplines, have different backgrounds, and possess different strengths and weaknesses, they share these four traits: ambition, discipline, self-awareness, and deliberate practice.

Adopt the traits and habits of top performers. Make them your own. As I describe each of these traits, honestly assess how you currently rate on a scale of 1 to 5, with 1 being nonexistent and 5 being very strong.

Ambition

"I've always been a competitive person. I needed to be top in my training class, which I was; next I wanted a house on a golf course, which I have; and then I wanted to be the number one salesperson in my firm, which I am." Those are the words of an elite sales professional whose ambition has enabled him to acquire wealth for himself and his family. Affluent sales pros establish serious annual goals—targets that often require them to venture outside their comfort zones and expand the depth and breadth of their knowledge. This tends to be an annual event. Every year these elite professionals set challenging goals directly linked to their overall ambitions.

Elite sales professionals have made their most important sale: They've sold themselves on the mind-set of a winner. They've acquired big goals and developed big plans. Deciding to move upmarket was instrumental in transforming these ambitions into reality.

- Rate your ambition: _____

Discipline

Whenever you encounter a top performer, you're in the presence of a disciplined professional. Top affluent salespeople do whatever is necessary, regardless of whether they'd rather be doing something else. It's not unusual to find them working on weekends, mixing business with pleasure, and attending social events that could lead to sales opportunities.

Because of this intense focus, fueled by ambition, these people work smart *and* hard. You'll find them working when they're tired, though they'll never admit to being tired. Unless they're hospitalized, you'll never see them miss work. They are constantly expanding their comfort zones by performing the required activities. They live Dr. Jeffers's mantra: Feel the fear and do it anyway.

- Rate your discipline: ____

Self-Awareness

This is what separates the elite from the rest. Self-aware individuals step back and honestly assess their strengths and weaknesses. You might think anyone can do this, and you're right. But few sales professionals actually do it. Why? Because humans are one of the few species, if not the only one, that rationalizes their behavior. Whether it's eating the dessert we should have skipped or failing to move upmarket when we claim that's what we want, we humans are good at justifying every action we choose to take or avoid.

This is not how elite affluent sales performers are wired. Top professionals are reading this book not necessarily because they want to move upmarket (they're already successful in affluent sales), but because they know they'll find a few nuggets of wisdom in this book. *That* is the spirit of self-awareness.

It was in this spirit that one of our coaches showcased a client, Gerry, at a recent workshop. Asked to stand and share with a group of more than 70 affluent sales professionals how self-awareness had immediately improved his sales, the young man explained that he was an estate-planning attorney who once talked too much and had to force himself, with the assistance of his coach, to actively listen. Gerry told a story of how an affluent prospect asked him a technical question regarding some estate issues. Even though he was well-versed in the topic, Gerry responded by asking the prospect, "Tell me what you already know." The prospect talked for 30 minutes. As it turned out, the prospect was extremely knowledgeable about his family's estate issues and estate planning in general. When he was done talking, the prospect said: "You really *are* an expert in estate planning." Gerry hadn't said a word, but at that moment he acquired a new affluent client. He did it through discipline and self-awareness.

Self-awareness can take the form of admitting fear, recognizing that you need to improve your image, or that you talk too much and listen too little. So, in the spirit of honestly assessing your affluent sales strengths and weaknesses . . .

- Rate your self-awareness: _____

Deliberate Practice

It takes practice to correct a weakness. Without self-awareness, however, there can be no *deliberate* practice. Correcting a weakness, any weakness, is never easy, and this is certainly true when it comes to correcting affluent sales weaknesses.

Gerry's strength was his legal expertise regarding complex estate issues. It was easy for him to discuss technical details, and he loved showcasing his knowledge. But it took a lot of work with his coach (deliberate practice) to recognize when he was talking too much. He had to practice pausing, listening, and then asking questions related to what the prospect or client had just said. As simple as this might appear, it was a serious challenge for Gerry. It's this trait—admitting and overcoming performance-specific weaknesses—that propels sales professionals to elite status.

Incidentally, you might be wondering why an estate-planning attorney hired an affluent sales coach. It was self-awareness linked to ambition. Gerry was in his early thirties, and wanted to be the top estate-planning attorney in town. For that to happen, he knew he needed to master the art of affluent selling. Kudos to Gerry!

How many attorneys are working on their affluent sales skills? Not many.

How many would like to have more business? Plenty.

It's easy to practice something at which you're already good. Working to correct a weakness is challenging. It involves failure, as does all learning. As rewarding as the practice will eventually prove, it's also a humbling experience, and that's a good thing. Humility pushes away arrogance, allowing us to accept new facts and new and improved ways of doing things.

• Rate your deliberate practice: _____

SUMMARY

Are you ready to put it all together? Are you ready to embark on your journey to personal affluence? If you've made it this far, the answer is probably "You bet I am!" Now it's a question of getting there—of applying what you've learned.

Those of you who read the first edition of *Mastering the Art of Selling to the Affluent* know that I like reminders. My philosophy revolves around these basic questions: How do you keep an honest person honest? How do you keep a disciplined person disciplined? How do you keep a motivated, goal-focused salesperson motivated and goal focused?

The first step in answering these questions is to look forward 12 months and envision the future you want to exist at that point. This will enable you to refocus your daily activity toward accomplishing what's important.

Envisioning your future is best accomplished by contrasting where you are now with where you want to be. This ensures that the gap between today and tomorrow becomes clear. Whichever items you include in your plan, you must be convinced that every one will pull you toward the future you've envisioned.

The next question focuses on how you will close the gaps you envisioned. Will your activities take the form of an avoidance pattern or an achievement pattern? You shape your daily activities into an achievement pattern when, instead of letting your negative and fear-driven feelings pull you off track, you focus on *doing*. Perform the FDAs that need to be done, regardless of what you're thinking or feeling at that moment.

Tackling the first FDA is always the toughest part, so conviction is important. You must believe that your goals are both realistic and achievable. As you perform the activities, your confidence builds. As you gain more experience, your competence grows.

Take time to revisit the four key traits of top affluent sales professionals. Let them serve as your framework for affluent sales success. Top affluent sales professionals do not get complacent.

It's no coincidence that affluence and hard work go hand in hand. The work is usually multifaceted: actual hours on the job, hours spent solving problems and handling service issues, and hours invested continually mastering a craft. The vast majority of affluent salespeople work far longer than those who aren't committed to affluence.

Research Facts

- Forty-five percent of affluent consumers say their income and job status have improved since the Great Recession, compared with 15 percent of nonaffluent consumers.
- Forty-three percent of affluent consumers claim their standard of living is better today than before the Great Recession, compared with 15 percent of nonaffluent consumers.
- Affluent households spend more than five times what their nonaffluent counterparts do ($167,332 vs. $28,039).
- Fifty-nine percent of affluent consumers have earned their standard of living in some form of sales career.
- Ninety-five percent of affluent consumers are self-made; only 2 percent inherited their wealth.

Taking Action

- Envision your future following the process outlined in this chapter.
- Repeat your goals at the beginning of each week—or daily, if it will help. Write them down and say them aloud over and over.

- Visualize your goals by sitting back, relaxing, and seeing yourself successfully completing the steps required to achieve each goal.
- Identify the FDAs needed to achieve your goals.
- Plan, schedule, perform, and measure these FDAs on a weekly basis.
- Be sure you are working hard *and* smart.
- Commit to acquiring and practicing the four traits of elite affluent sales professionals.

Appendix: The 12 Commandments of Affluent Selling

Personal service and problem solving are key factors in strengthening loyalty among affluent consumers.
                                        —Factoid, 2013 APD Research

COMMANDMENT 1: BE TOTALLY COMMITTED

You must be ambitious to master the art of affluent selling. It takes a lot of work, and much of that work will force you outside your comfort zone. You will be required to undertake specific activities while the devilish voice whispers sabotaging thoughts in your ear. In short, it's unlikely you'll achieve personal affluence without being totally committed to your goals.

Do not *assume* that you're committed. This assumption has derailed many a sales career. It's been my experience that top affluent sales professionals are always looking for new ways to reinforce their commitment—new ways to stay engaged and motivated while traveling the critical path. This is why I've listed *total commitment* as the first commandment. Unless you're one of the 2 percent of Americans who will inherit their wealth, the journey to personal affluence requires total commitment.

Commit to yourself and to your career. Believe in both, regardless of what anyone tells you. Nothing can replace your passion— that sheer force of positive energy you bring to your profession. You must love your job and trust in your passion to excel in your career.

I know salespeople who love their jobs, but aren't committed to maximizing their potential. For them, the job merely enables them to make a living. For you, the job is a heartfelt commitment that will enable you to create a life of affluence. There's a huge difference. Total commitment is the fuel that inspires you to work hard and work smart. It provides you with the personal power that inspires trust, makes you believable, and increases your magnetic pull in affluent circles. It serves as the motivation behind all the learning and professional development you have undertaken and will continue to pursue. Commitment is the tonic that helps drown out that devilish voice of doubt and keeps you doing what needs to be done when you feel like doing something else. All true greatness is born of total commitment. Everyone loves a winner. The self-made people who comprise 93 percent of our 2013 APD Research respondents love dealing with people who are cut from the same cloth.

Today's cynical affluent can easily spot the difference between a salesperson who's totally committed and someone going through the motions. They are attracted to your commitment, your professionalism, and your responsiveness, and they are repelled by those whose hearts aren't in the job. I'm sure you are too. We encounter these people all time, but usually they're in dead-end jobs, in which case their commitment should be to improve themselves enough to qualify for more lucrative positions. It's a shame that many professionals are capable of so much more, but they fail to advance because of their lack of commitment.

Commitment is a form of personal energy, and it's contagious. People are attracted to those who are committed to excellence in the same way they're attracted to people with positive energy. When affluent consumers see you as a committed professional who is responsive to their needs and goal-focused, they'll be more likely to conduct business with you rather than the competition. At the same time, you have to be yourself—the real you. You must be comfortable with who you are personally and professionally. Affluent consumers do not like poseurs.

Personal development is a form of personal commitment that fuels step-by-step action. Few people enjoy a lifetime of health and fitness because of their genes. Most have to take appropriate step-by-step actions: They exercise regularly and eat properly. This has a positive impact on their attitude and behavior. They feel better about themselves, they eat better, exercise regularly, are moderate in their consumption of alcohol, and are careful to get their proper allotment of sleep.

A total commitment to your career will activate similar positives in your life. You'll feel better about yourself, you'll perform better, earn more, and grow personally and professionally as a result. I've never seen affluent sales success produced by casual effort. Never! You've got to actively seek it. You have to proactively locate affluent prospects. They won't walk up to you and say, "I want to be your client." You commit to finding them. If that means overcoming affluent call reluctance, reread Chapter 11 and work through the exercises. To master the art of selling to the affluent, you must become part of who they are and what they do.

If you have any questions about the importance of developing relationships with today's affluent, revisit Chapter 5. Reread the sections on "Getting Personal" and "Becoming Social" because, if you're truly totally committed, you'll discover that none of this is difficult.

You've got to be the real deal at all times. Whenever you are face-to-face with prospective affluent customers, if you aren't committed to excellence, it's unlikely you'll be taken seriously by the affluent. It's important, therefore, to improve your appearance (if need be) and to start hobnobbing with the affluent in your community. Remain true to who you are while becoming laser-focused on where you want to go.

Linking goals to acquiring affluence is what 96 percent of today's affluent consumers have experienced on a personal level. Not only do they understand what you're trying to accomplish, but they also respect it.

COMMANDMENT 2: BE AS ADVERTISED

My wife Sandy recently switched our personal Internet provider. As you may know, this is a convoluted affair. Internet and cable services are now bundled, making it difficult to determine how much you pay for which service. In our case, Time Warner was making house calls in our neighborhood. Why? A little over a year ago AT&T laid cable in the area and made a strong pitch for the quality of their services. Unhappy with Time Warner, we were one of many households to switch providers.

A little over a year later, AT&T has more than doubled their rates. Aware of the dissatisfaction, Time Warner has embarked on a campaign to recapture lost clients. Sandy was skeptical at first, but after two face-to-face meetings with the young lady who rang our doorbell, she was assured she could get the connectivity she needed—specifically, in her sunroom.

Two months later, we still have no Time Warner connectivity. The technician who came to assess the problem told Sandy that it wasn't possible to get connectivity in her sunroom. Sandy replied "I was told by your rep that I would definitely *have* connectivity." The Time Warner technician replied, "I don't care what you were told or by whom, you can't get connectivity in your sunroom."

Truth in advertising has become such a sore subject at home that I don't even ask about our Internet provider anymore.

Do you recall the last time you purchased an item or paid for a professional service that was not everything it claimed to be? I'll bet you can.

GM and Ford are making miraculous comebacks from the brink of disaster. They have streamlined, have started making better automobiles, and are rekindling efforts to recapture portions of the luxury car market they lost to the German and Japanese competition. It's going to be a long haul. They've attempted this before, but they cut corners on the actual products while sparing no expense on advertising. Because their products didn't measure up to the German and Japanese models, negative word-of-mouth severely damaged their reputations. It's no wonder that our 2013 APD Research respondents give the automotive industry a 42 percent trust factor regarding their advertising.

Assuming Detroit is finally creating luxury automobiles that can compete, they'd better carve off some advertising dollars to stimulate positive word-of-mouth influence within affluent circles.

Banks have also returned to profitability and, though they rate slightly better than the automotive companies with a 49 percent trust factor, they too are suffering from a lack of trust among the affluent. Although our research tells us that affluent consumers would rather have one professional oversee their family's financial affairs, the individual financial advisor has a 44 percent trust factor, with the affluent female even more distrustful (with a 36 percent trust factor). Once again, a quick glance at the advertising of financial services firms reveals a disconnect between the messages and the reality.

Your product better be as advertised, your services better be as advertised, and you, the professional sales consultant, need to be aware of all this—not only as it relates to your product or service, but also as it relates to your competition. Your word must be your bond. According to my wife, "[Time Warner] probably took advantage of that poor saleswoman. I'm sure she wouldn't lie, but I'll bet they lied to her." She's since changed her tone, as this "poor saleswoman" hasn't returned her phone calls. Who knows what happened in this instance. Whatever happened, it's unlikely that this salesperson received any affluent sales training.

Be as promised. Always follow through. Help resolve problems. This is what stimulates positive word-of-mouth influence. And if, God forbid, you find yourself being asked to sell a product or service that isn't what it's cracked up to be, follow this commandment and at least your personal reputation will remain intact. Your reputation is all you have. Treat it like gold.

COMMANDMENT 3: BE A PROBLEM SOLVER

Affluent loyalty means everything. It leads to ongoing business (repeat purchases) and positive word-of-mouth influence. Ninety-three percent of our 2013 APD Research respondents rated *problems resolved quickly* as a key factor in conducting ongoing business. Problems occur every day, and the affluent place a premium on those who help them resolve those problems.

Nobody expects perfection. Even the affluent understand that things go wrong, mistakes are made, and products and services sometimes fail to perform as promised. They recognize that Murphy's Law is a powerful force. The secret to affluent success is doing something about problems when they occur. Your mission is to be a go-to problem-solver.

Here's a perfect example of a good and a not-so-good problem-solver. Both cases involve home repairs in affluent neighborhoods. The good problem-solver was called to repair a leaky air conditioner that caused sheetrock damage to the ceiling below. This technician responded within 30 minutes of the call, fixed the leak, and contacted another contractor to repair the damaged sheetrock. He was immediately put on contract for biannual inspection of the two AC units in the home. The sheetrock repair crew were apparently made of the same stuff. They noticed that the gutters were clogged, and proceeded to clean them while waiting for the sheetrock to dry. This story, along with the contractors' contact information, has gone viral in the neighborhood. Solving a problem is a key component in affluent loyalty.

Confused? Don't be. I just had a conversation with a perfect stranger sitting next to me on a flight to Phoenix that epitomized this commandment. He told me a sad tale about the tenth luxury car that he'd purchased; same make and same dealer. In his words, "My beautiful automobile was only two weeks old when a taxi rear-ended me at a red light." His rear bumper was damaged, requiring a new bumper, but his car had an exotic type of paint that was difficult to match. It took the dealer more than two months to complete his bumper repair. Meanwhile, the dealer never offered a replacement luxury car (the client was sent to a rental car agency).

Being a longstanding affluent client, he voiced his complaints to the company's North America senior executive. All he received was an apology; nothing happened. "He said all the right things, but nothing happened. All he needed to do was loan me a comparable vehicle while my car was in the shop—if, in addition, he had done something special, like give me a gift certificate to the special driving school this manufacturer runs, I'd still be driving their cars."

It's been eight years and not only has he never purchased another vehicle of that brand, he's told his story to everyone who will listen.

As he told me, all that was required was someone to proactively solve his problem, beyond the bumper, without his asking, and he'd still be driving their vehicles. Ouch!

The not-so-good problem-solvers were involved in a kitchen renovation. This was a major assignment, so a Who's Who of home repairmen streamed in and out of our house all day. We wondered how many times the expert carpenters and handymen would struggle with a tricky doorknob in need of a simple adjustment and how many would take the initiative to fix it.

Answer: zero.

Being a problem-solver means going beyond the call of duty. It means exceeding expectations, and doing so with a smile. You, as the salesperson and the first line of contact, are the person who must make certain all problems are solved in this fashion.

I know you didn't sign up to be a gofer to affluent clients. However, you *do* want to assist them in any way possible. Referring an affluent client who's going on vacation to a reputable dog sitter doesn't take much effort, but it solves a problem that may pay for itself many times over.

Solving a solved problem is the high-octane fuel that propels word-of-mouth influence.

When it comes to major purchase decisions, affluent consumers will remember and talk about the problems they encountered. Resolve them quickly and to their satisfaction, and they will sing your praises.

COMMANDMENT 4: BE A SERVANT

Ninety-five percent of respondents in our 2013 APD Research cite *good service* as a key factor in continuing to use a service provider or making repeat purchases. Patel has proved this beyond all doubt. He's provided such exceptional service at an Exxon station that it's become the affluent go-to destination for gas.

Earning the loyalty of an affluent clientele requires a combination of all 12 commandments. Solving a problem is key to stimulating word-of-mouth influence and strengthening loyalty, but if it's not coupled with outstanding service it's unlikely that loyalty will strengthen over the long haul. The idea is to make a personal commitment to providing the level of personalized service that wows today's affluent. A blend of personal service and problem solving is the best formula for gaining affluent loyalty and positive word-of-mouth.

In my travels I'm always taking note of exceptional service. It's easy to notice because it's so rare. When I ask lecture audiences to recall an exceptional service experience, it usually produces an "Ah-ha!" moment. They realize that the positive experience was something they shared with others and, most important, they realize that it didn't require much effort.

Be a servant. Always go that extra mile to deliver personalized service.

These little things will distinguish you from your competitors. Excellent service is greatly appreciated, remembered, and discussed.

COMMANDMENT 5: BE A TRUSTED SOURCE OF INFORMATION

Before affluent consumers make a big purchase, they usually do their homework. They consult with people who are knowledgeable in that area, they personally inspect the product or service, they conduct online research, and they listen to the opinions and recommendations of people they respect and trust. In short, they arm themselves with information.

This is what makes affluent consumers seem confident in their decision making. They search diligently for the information needed to make major decisions, especially major financial decisions. You can't provide all of the information, but you must be a reliable source for some. They are smart enough to know when a given source is unreliable or misleading. Once the affluent discover that you can be trusted, they will be drawn to you like a magnet.

Your depth and breadth of knowledge must go beyond that of your own products and services. We're now immersed in a digital age of information overload. You need to know everything you can about your direct competitors, your industry, and any alternatives to what you're offering, for example, the pros and cons of purchasing a second home at the beach versus a timeshare. You must consider yourself a knowledge worker—someone who can assist well-informed consumers in making the decisions that are best for them.

Because affluent consumers have little faith in most advertising, you're well-positioned to become a knowledgeable voice of truth. Yes, this requires more work now than at any time in the history of capitalism. But the rewards are waiting for you. Remember, the largest segment of affluent consumers acquires their wealth through some form of sales.

COMMANDMENT 6: PROVIDE VALUE THAT EXCEEDS PRICE

Today's affluent expect a big purchase to perform as advertised. It's a *minimal* expectation. You can't distinguish yourself simply by believing that your product or service is better than your competition's. As I explained in Chapter 4 on affluent buzz, positive word-of-mouth among today's cynical affluent is stimulated by exceeding expectations.

I love that old cliché "price is only a consideration in the absence of value," because in today's commoditized world, value is increasingly elusive. This is where master affluent salespeople enter at center stage. They recognize that face-to-face interaction is the preferred method of communication for complex transactions, which is why they go out of their way to meet with clients and prospects personally. Meanwhile, the average salesperson doesn't think face-to-face interactions are necessary, and too often relies on email or the phone.

Finding the lowest price ranks seventh on our list of 10 factors driving final purchase decisions. Make no mistake: Price *is* important to affluent consumers. After all, they've worked hard to afford these purchases. What's more, everyone loves a deal, including the affluent. However, when it comes to major decisions, value always trumps the lowest price. Whether it's an M series BMW or an 18-karat gold Cartier watch, there are a many luxury items available at those price points. Therefore, many purchase decisions are driven by the extent to which the perceived value exceeds the price—value that is frequently generated by the master salesperson.

Never overcharge affluent consumers. They *will* learn the truth, and negative word-of-mouth will be the result. However, affluent customers *will* pay a competitive price for what they want.

I realize that online shopping has everyone focused on the best price, but remember: We're talking about *exceeding* expectations, and lowest price ranks low on the affluent list of expectations. You must articulate your value clearly and sincerely to every prospect with whom you come in contact. As one salesperson recently said, "I remind my clients and tell every prospect that 'nobody is going to look out for you the way I will.'" I could tell that she meant every word of this.

COMMANDMENT 7: DISCLOSE ALL COSTS

Airlines are making millions by adding on fees. Check your luggage? Add an additional fee. Want more leg room? Another charge. Want to be guaranteed that you will not be sitting in a middle seat? Still another charge. Yet people continue to fly and, despite the high cost of fuel, the airlines are earning big profits.

Today's affluent, who represent the majority of airline passengers (counting their children), will pay these fees as long as they're fully disclosed. Problems arise, though, when they discover a fee that was never disclosed—a discovery that immediately earns their distrust. Whether the lack of disclosure was an innocent oversight or a deliberate attempt to mislead, whatever trust existed between the affluent consumer and the salesperson (as well as the company) has been seriously damaged. Overcharging the affluent isn't a good idea, as it will stimulate negative word-of-mouth, but it doesn't even come close to breaching trust with affluent buyers.

Although affluent consumers are a skeptical species, they *will* pay your price, especially if you adhere to the first six commandments.

If you live in a world of intangibles—that is, if you sell services—it's critical that you clearly communicate the value you're delivering for the price. Neglecting to initiate a discussion about fees simply because your affluent client didn't ask is a huge faux pas. This is one of those areas in which insurance agents, financial advisors, lawyers, CPAs, and high-end Realtors must be extremely careful. Their fees are often complex, frequently high, and difficult to explain. As a result, there is a tendency to avoid fee discussions whenever possible.

As a service provider, please don't fall into that trap. Your clients are willing to pay. They aren't looking for a discount cardiologist to put a stint in grandpa's heart. And they're not looking for a discounted CPA to help them minimize the taxes they pay to Uncle Sam.

COMMANDMENT 8: STAND BY EVERYTHING

Our 2013 APD Research respondents put *warranty* center stage, ranking it in the top-five factors influencing the final decision to purchase and among the top-three factors when it comes to influencing repeat purchases. In our 2004 APD Research, we gave respondents the opportunity to write in other criteria they considered important when making major purchase decisions. Of all the items listed in that section, warranty/guarantee was the most frequent. Today, affluent consumers have made it official—you'd better stand by everything!

You mission is this: Stand behind everything you sell and make sure your warranty/guarantee is clearly understood. A faulty warranty or one that deceptively absolves the manufacturer of responsibility in fine print will create a major problem. Trust will vanish and negative word-of-mouth influence will commence.

Your clients understand that you have little control over corporate policy—that you have nothing to do with creating guarantees and warranties. They also realize that many companies offer extended warranties to create add-on sales. Your clientele will expect you to know your warranty inside and out, and if an extended warranty is available, they will expect you to do more than pressure them to buy it. They will expect you to explain its costs and benefits.

Communication and clarity are the main issue. Since consumers want informed assistance in making their decisions, be sure to spend time explaining everything carefully and, based on what you have learned about your clientele, provide an honest recommendation regarding options to extend the warranty period. Patel's parting remark to a customer who had just purchased an expensive set of headphones, "If you don't like them you can always being them back," is a perfect example of this commandment in action.

COMMANDMENT 9: YOU *ARE* THE FIRM

In the complex world of affluent tax preparation, CPAs understand that *they* are the product. The same goes for financial planners: Financial plans are the output and, with obvious variations, each professional's product is roughly the same. When it comes to intangibles, the professional *is* the product as far as affluent consumers are concerned. To a lesser extent, the same is true of tangible product providers. Whether you're selling a $25,000 entertainment system or a luxury automobile, affluent consumers will associate you with the products.

What this means is that you are responsible for solving any and all problems, for maximizing the utility of the purchase, and for helping consumers navigate your organization. This is why it's important to be familiar with your company's website, its promotional offerings, and the operations of your service department.

It pays to develop a good relationship with both your firm's technical support and service department. One of our coaches has a financial advisor who takes her entire team of five for a Las Vegas weekend whenever they meet their six-month targets. This weekend serves to refocus and recommit everyone to hitting the team's 12-month goals. Upon hitting those 12-month targets, everyone gets a bonus in addition to another weekend in Las Vegas.

Las Vegas wouldn't be my choice, but apparently it works for them. The idea is to get everyone, support and service included, working with you to achieve the same goals.

COMMANDMENT 10: COVET YOUR REPUTATION

As you've probably noticed, these commandments build on one another. Among other things, their cumulative effect enhances your reputation. Follow the principles I've outlined, and your reputation will be your greatest sales tool.

Word-of-mouth influence and reputation go hand-to-glove in the world of the affluent. This is why so much of your success revolves around word-of-mouth influence.

When it comes to reputation, everything about you counts—professional *and* personal. All of your behavior matters. If you make a fool of yourself at a social function, cut in line at the local Starbucks, or stiff the valet parking attendant at a local restaurant, the incongruence with your professional image will damage your reputation. Mastering the art of affluent sales requires around-the-clock attention to detail. You must be committed 24/7, but it's well worth the effort.

COMMANDMENT 11: BECOME SOCIAL MEDIA AND INTERNET SAVVY

When I wrote the first edition of *The Art of Selling to the Affluent*, this commandment was about the Internet. It's amazing how quickly things change in the digital world. Nowadays, it seems everyone is online. Everyone is Internet savvy and cell phones are standard equipment.

The affluent of all ages are embracing social media faster than their nonaffluent counterparts. Thirty-five percent of our 2013 APD Research respondents told us that they have connected with service providers through LinkedIn, compared with just 10 percent of nonaffluent respondents. Fifty-nine percent of nonaffluent consumers don't used LinkedIn, compared with 29 percent of the affluent.

More and more people are using social media, and the affluent are leading the charge, which is why you'll need a working knowledge of sites like LinkedIn, Twitter, YouTube, and so forth, and a working knowledge of how affluent clients use them.

If you aren't certain of what all that means, take steps to find out. You will also want to use social media and the Internet as tools that to assist you in doing research on clients, prospects, and your competition. Understanding your competition, obtaining personal information about clients and prospects, and getting a glimpse of their social media Rolodexes are all important to mastering affluent sales in today's digital world. Remember, today's affluent are "wired"—digitally connected through their smartphones, computers, iPads—and the emerging affluent are even more wired.

You'll want more than just a website. You'll need to be a master of the Google search. This involves inserting specific keywords and phrases throughout your online profiles, particularly on LinkedIn, since it's the site most often used by professionals. Your brand can be impacted positively or negatively by your social media presence.

Be careful with whom you connect: Connections to fraternity brothers who are now cage fighters won't enhance your brand, and connecting with competitors gives them to access your new-age Rolodex.

Today's affluent do a tremendous amount of prepurchase research. They are Internet savvy and active on social media. Offering your thoughts on your field of expertise, not just your products or services, via LinkedIn, Twitter, and YouTube, can increase your appeal among today's affluent. When you become social media savvy, you take the Internet to the next level.

COMMANDMENT 12: NO HASSLES

Solving a problem for an affluent client remains one of the best ways to strengthen loyalty. Conversely, nothing drives an affluent client to your competition faster than multiple problems. Your mantra should revolve around this twelfth commandment: Clients will endure no hassles.

Whether it's Patel checking the tire pressure for a customer or promising "If you don't like X you can bring it back," there are many ways to eliminate hassles large and small.

Because most of today's affluent (well over 90 percent) worked hard to achieve their affluent lifestyle, they have little time or patience for unnecessary hassles, especially when it comes to making major purchases. Ritz-Carlton-quality service delivered with FedEx efficiency is critical to developing client loyalty. If you also exceed their expectations via surprise and delight, your affluent buzz factor kicks into high gear. Remember: Affluent women spread the word more quickly and are considered more credible sources of opinions and recommendations.

This is all about your affluent buzz. By eliminating hassles, you create and maintain a positive affluent buzz about you and your services. Your affluent clients *want* to be loyal. Why? Because it reduces the amount of hassle in their lives.

Look at the section in Chapter 3 in which I asked you to review your service experience. Where can you fine tune your service experience to deliver more than what's expected? If you want to take a deeper dive into this topic, make a list of every affluent prospect and client you encountered over the past 30 days, and determine your points of contact before, during, and after the sale. Beside each contact point, write down anything that might test the patience of a busy affluent prospect, customer, or client. You know what to do next: Eliminate those problems so that dealing with you becomes a hassle-free experience.

Eliminate hassles for prospects, and they're much more likely to become clients. Eliminate hassles for clients and they will make certain that your affluent buzz is loud and clear.

In my view, mastering these 12 commandments is the equivalent of earning a PhD in affluence. To attain personal affluence, you must become a lifetime student of the affluent. You must know their likes, dislikes, pet peeves, how they make buying decisions, what influences them, their ego defenses, how hard they work, the stress in their lives—everything. In many respects, you must come to know them better than they know themselves.

Refer to these commandments as a reminder.

Reread the chapters when you need a review.

Master the art of selling to the affluent and enjoy your journey to personal affluence.

Index

A

Accessories:
  men's attire and, 109
  of top performers, 105–106
  women's attire and, 110
Achievement cycle:
  activating, 201–202
  goal commitment (subconscious
    imprinting), 204
  goal-focused action steps,
    204–206
  past, 202–204
Achievement pattern activities, 119,
  199, 200, 207, 216
Acknowledgment, of prospect's
  comments, 64, 65
Action phase, in sales reluctance,
  183
Action plan, developing, 14

Action steps, for "wow" service
  experience, 31
Activating achievement cycle,
  201–202
Activating buzz factor, 49–54
Act of kindness, committing to, 40
Advertised, being as, 222–224
Advertising/advertisement:
  affluent consumers and, 17
  awareness of, 25
  campaigns, impact on affluents,
    18–19
  mistrust in, 121–122
  spending, 20
  trust in, 7, 19, 80–81,
    118–119, 150
  truth in, 222–223, 227
Affluent Purchasing Decision (APD)
  Research, 12

Affluents. *See also* Emerging
    affluents; Working affluents
  buzz, methods for creating, 43,
    50–62
  criteria of, 5–6
  household income of, 6
  investable assets of, 6
  macro shifts, 7–8
  older, 137, 139
  profile of today's, 5–6
  standard of living of, 24
Affluents sales opportunity:
  achievement cycle, 201–206
  closing the gap, 199–201, 216
  envisioning your future, 195–
    199, 216
  traits of top affluent sales
    professionals, 212–216
Airlines, 87–88, 135
Amazon, 152
Amazon Effect, 39
  Apple Experience, 150–151
  as factor in purchase decision,
    147–150
  online research, 151–158
  research facts, 158–159
  taking action, 159
Ambition, 213, 219
America's contemporary dress
    codes, 104
Appearance, of salespeople, 112
Apple experience, 150–151
Apple store, 99
Appreciation, expressing, 48–49
Assertiveness, salespeople and, 67
Assessment, of earning potential, 174
Assets, management of, 3
AT&T, 21, 222
Attendees, following up with, 54
Attire:
  appropriate, 98, 99, 105
  men's, 104, 108–109, 110–111
  salesperson, 107
  women's, 104, 109–110
Attitudes, of affluents, 4, 5

Attitude shift, of affluents, 7
Automotive industry:
  advertising in 2011, 20, 25
  digital technology and, 134–135
  trust in advertising, 19, 223
Auto-themed event, 45–46
Avoidance pattern activities, 119,
    199, 200, 207, 216

B
Banks, trust in advertising, 19
BMW, 75, 92, 134, 228
Body language, 98, 103, 106
Body piercings, 106
Books, as gifts, 36
Boomers, 133
Branding, 107
Brands, 124, 142
Brochures, handing out, 68
Brooks Brothers, 105
Buick, 20
Building relationships, 9
Business-and-personal relationship,
    positive client attitudes and,
    7–8
Business cards, handing out, 68
Business conversation, expanding to
    personal, 92
Business dress, of top performers,
    105
Business paths, to engage partners,
    83
Business relationship, 76, 78
Business-social relationship, 86–87
Buzz and Wow. *See* Wow and buzz
Buzz factor. *See also* Intimate
    events; Social media; Visibility
    campaign
  activating, 49–54
  Apple store and, 99–100
  auto-themed event, 45–46
  avoiding large-scale client events,
    46–48
  getting involved, 62–63
  methods for creating, 43–44

objectives, 48–50
purchase decision and, 148
research facts and taking action, 70–71
revisiting past opportunities, 66–69
social prospecting, 64–66
starting, 43–45

C
Capital, moving upmarket and, 172
Career, commitment to, 220–222
Carnegie, Dale, 103, 104, 107
Carney, Dana, 102
Cell phone companies, trust in advertising, 19
Cell phones:
exchanging numbers of, 68, 71, 85
trust in advertising, 19
Challenges:
facing affluent sales, 163
of managing relationships, 82–83
of social prospecting, 64
Charitable events, 51
Cialdini, Robert, 32
Citysearch, 153
Client appreciation events. See Large-scale client events
Clients, 130
action steps for "wow" service experience with, 31
communication with, 89–90
developing plan for, 14
event checklist, 57, 58
identifying, 45, 143
inventory of, 13
large-scale events, 46–48
relationship with, 7–8, 25
salespersons interfacing with, 106
selecting, 50
surprise and delight initiative, 31–32
uncovering information about, 34–39

Closing deals, 5
Cold calling, 64
Comfort zone, 195, 199, 202
Commandments of affluent selling:
be as advertised, 222–224
be a servant, 226–227
be a trusted source of information, 227
become social media and Internet savvy, 232–233
be covetous of your reputation, 231–232
be problem solver, 224–226
be totally commitment, 219–222
disclose all costs, 229–230
no hassles, 233–234
provide value that exceeds price, 228–229
stand by everything, 230
you are the firm, 231
Commissions, 198
Commitment, 195
to act of kindness, 40
affluent sales and, 232
goal, 204
total, 219–222
Communication:
adjusting to each generation, 143
with affluent clients, 89–90
with the emerging affluent, 139–140
face-to-face, 93, 113, 143, 228
good first impression and, 98
personalized, 140
preferred medium of, 113
style preferences, 127
Community groups, 63
Company reputation, 150
Compelling reason introduction approach, 79
Competence, 206
Competition:
online monitoring of, 142
reviewing online presence of, 143

Computer companies, trust in
 advertising, 19
Confidence:
 in achieving future, 198
 building, 205–206
 in financial advisors, 3, 8
 salespersons and earning, 5
Confirmation/invitation note, 53
Congressional Budget Office
 (CBO), 6, 13
Connecting, with females of
 households, 128–129
Connections:
 affluent social media, 199
 uncovering, 71
Consumer behavior, Amazon Effect
 and, 156
Consumers, affluent:
 association with products, 231
 digitized, 88–89
 factors influencing purchase
  decisions, 141, 150
 faith in advertising, 227
 investment and purchase
  decisions of, 3–4
 mind-set of, 17–19
 online research and, 143,
  151–158
Consumers, nonaffluent:
 income/job status, 23, 217
 online research and, 151–158
 online reviews and, 153
 retreat from stock and real estate
  markets and stores, 4
 standard of living of, 24
Contrast, items to, 197–199
Convenience/ease of purchase,
 as purchase decision factor,
 148–149
Conversation:
 engaging in, 83, 118
 enhancing, 91, 94
 expanding from business to
  personal, 92

salespeople and, 65–66
Conviction, 205
Cornell University white paper,
 136–137
Costs, disclosing, 229–230
Creating events, 50–52
Credibility, events and establishing,
 48–50
Critical path, concept of, 206–207
Critical Path Organizer:
 analyzing weekly activity, 212
 daily planning, 197, 207, 212
 measuring weekly activity,
  211, 212
 weekly planning, 207, 209–210
CRM system, 92
Cuddy, Amy, 102
Cultural events, 51
Current, staying, 141

D
Daily activities/planning, 197,
 207, 212
Decision making:
 of emerging affluents, 136–139
 pre- and post-crisis, 21–23
 process, online reviews and,
  152–153
Deliberate practice, 215–216
Delight. See Surprise and delight
Dell computers, 151
Demographics, adopting social
 media, 70
Dialogue, opening, 141–142
Digital photos, memorializing
 events with, 54, 59–60
Digital promotions, 199
Digital technology, 134
Digitized affluent consumers, 88–89
Direct introduction approach, 79
Discipline, 213–214
Distrust in advertising, 24.
 See also Trust
"Dress for success" (Molloy), 98, 108

Dress for success principles, 107, 108–111
Drug companies:
    Pfizer spending on advertising, 20
    trust in advertising, 19
Dudley, George, 178–179, 190
Dunkin Donuts, 97

E
Earnings, household, 13, 133
Ease of returning/refund, as factor in purchase decisions, 150
eBay, 111
Education, of affluents, 13, 19, 167
Educational events, 51
80/20 rule, 34–35
Elite sales professionals, 213, 214
E-mails:
    communication, 89, 93
    Millennial generation and, 135, 143
    sending to attendees, 61
Embarrassment, fear of, 173
Emerging affluents:
    communication and, 139–140
    decision making of, 136–139
    digital technology and, 134–135
    generational divide, 133–135
    generational similarities, 141–142
    research facts, 142–143
    taking action, 143
    word-of-mouth power through social media, 135–136
Energy, personal, 98
Entertainment, 51
Environment:
    checklist, 112, 113
    first impression and impact of, 99–100, 112
Envisioning your future, 195–199, 216
Events. See also Intimate events
    checklist, 57–59
    clients, large-scale, 46–48

conducting, 53–54
creating right, 50–52
debrief, 60
following up with attendees, 54
invitation process, 52–53
life, major, 35
planning form, 55–56
preferred by affluent clients, 70
Expertise, reassessing, 14

F
Facebook, 43, 90, 135, 136, 143
Face-to-face communication, 93, 113, 143, 228
Face-to-face contacts, 200, 207, 208
Face-to-face interactions, 70, 105, 228
Fear:
    as challenge to affluent sales, 163
    maximizing potential and, 172
    overcoming, 165
    worst exercise, 172–173
FedEx, 233
Feeling-thinking-doing, 202
Feel the Fear and Do It Anyway (Jeffers), 172
Female of the household:
    action plan for knowing, 14
    building relationships with, 9
    connecting with, 128–129, 130
    developing rapport with, 118
    impact on purchase decisions, 117–118
    influence of, 117
    phoning, 127
    role in family finances, 7
Financial advisors:
    faith and confidence in, 3
    female *vs.* male attitudes toward, 119–121
    ratings of, 8
    redirecting social contact, 65
    trust in, 3, 9, 19

Financial crisis:
  income status since, 24
  population segments and, 23
Financial professional performance
    rankings, 86–87
First impression:
  environment and, 99–100, 112
  factors creating, 97–99
  impact of Great Recession,
    97–99
  making good, 103–105, 110
  personal presence and, 100–101
  personal tips, 105–112
  power pose and, 101–103
  research facts, 112–113
  taking action, 113
  trying hard to make, 67–68
Fixed daily activities (FDAs), 200,
    204, 207, 216–217, 218
Focus, 22
Follow-up, pushy, 69
Food/beverage companies, trust in
    advertising, 19
Forbes, 124
Ford, 223
Frank, Robert, 166
Freeman, Karen, 149
Future, envisioning your,
    195–199, 216

G
Gaps, closing, 199–201, 216
Gender shift, 7, 129, 148
Generational age breakdown,
    133–135
Generation X, 133, 138, 143, 148
Getting back on track technique, 186
"The Gift of Gab: Women and
    Word of Mouth Advocacy"
    (Keller), 124
Gifts:
  for enhancing vacations
    experience, 35
  with lasting impact, selecting, 35
  linking to special event, 34
    for major life events, 35
    personal, 32, 33
    on personalized products, 36
    wow factor, 36–37
"Give Yourself 5 Stars? Online, It
    Might Cost You" (Streitfeld),
    153
"Giving Mom 's Book Five Stars?
    Amazon May Cull Your
    Review" (Streitfeld), 152
GM, 20, 223
Goal(s):
  action steps focused on,
    204–206
  commitment (subconscious
    imprinting), 204
  doing activities and, 202
  focus, 169
  repeating, 204, 217
  visualizing, 204, 218
Goodson, Shannon, 178, 190
Google, 153
Google/Keller Fay Group, 59, 70
Google search, 233
Great Recession:
  affluent view of sales and
    marketing, 80
  impact of, 97–99
  income/job status of affluents,
    217
  purchase decisions and, 3, 4, 7,
    13, 117
Grooming of top performers, 106
Groups:
  joining, 62–63
  targeting members of, 71
"Group think" approach, 134
Guests, intimate events and, 70

H
Hassles, eliminating, 233–234
"Hearts, Minds, and Choices:
    Helping Improve Decision-
    Making Across the Life Span"
    (Reed), 137

Helmstetter, Shad, 201, 202
High power posers, 103
Hirschfield, Michael, 18
Honest appreciation, 103
Hosting intimate event, 45–46
Household income, 6
Households, affluent. *See also*
    Female of the household
    earning of, 13, 133
    income of, 12, 13
    net worth of of average, 174
    spending of, 174
"How 'Power Poses' Can Help Your
    Career" (Shellenbarger), 102
*How to Win Friends and Influence
    People* (Carnegie), 103

I
Income:
    of affluents since Great
        Recession, 217
    contrasting monthly, 198
    financial crisis and, 23
    of male and female, 23
Infiniti, 171
Influence. *See* Spheres of influence
*Influence: The Psychology of
    Persuasion* (Cialdini), 32
Information. *See also* Personal
    information
    on attendees, gathering, 40, 54
    client, uncovering, 34–39
    in periodicals, 155
    source, being trusted as, 227
    tracker, client, 37–38
Initial call, in invitation process,
    52–53
Insurance firms, trust in advertising
    in, 19
Intelligence gathering:
    alternative methods of, 35
    basic information, 37–38
    personal, 33, 34, 38
Interactions, preferred
    communication for, 89

Interest in other people, 103
Internet:
    selling commandment and
        embracing, 232–233
    smart phone owners and, 70
Intimate events:
    activating affluent buzz via,
        50–58
    fun, scheduling, 71
    to generate buzz, 43
    hosting, 45–46
    mastering invitation process,
        52–53
    objectives of, 48–50
    planning form, 55–60
    as preferred event of affluents, 70
    specific ideas, 51–52
    types of, 51
Introduction:
    to affluent prospects, 198
    personal, 49
    referrals *vs.*, 77–81
Inventory, of clients, 13, 130
Investable assets, 6, 12, 13
Investment decisions, 3–4
Investor perception, of client
    events, 48
Invitation process, 52–53, 71
Irregular timing, employing, 34

J
Jeffers, Susan, 172, 214
Jewelers, 87
Job status, 23, 24, 217

K
Kantar Media, 20, 25
Keller, Ed, 124
Keller Fay Group, 124
KIA, 171
Kimpton Hotels, 128
Knowledge
    lack of, salesperson and, 125, 174
    of products and services, 14, 174
    working affluent and, 170

L

Language, using the right, 67
Large-scale client events, 46–48
Lasting impression, 107
Law of reciprocity, 32–33, 43
Leondakis, Niki, 128
Lexus, 134, 171
Life events, major, 35
Life milestone events, 51
Lifestyle:
    of men and women, 24
    pre-and post-crisis, 23–24
LinkedIn, 90, 94, 113, 232, 233
List creation, of past
    opportunities, 66
Listening, 103, 126
L.L. Bean, 140
Loyalty:
    affluent, 224, 226
    personalizing business
        relationships and, 39
    strengthening, 46, 49, 233

M

Madoff, Bernie, 4
Manners, displaying good, 107
Marketing strategies, 124
McCartney, Scott, 87
Meece, Mickey, 129
Men, affluent
    attire of, 104, 108–109, 110–111
    attitudes toward financial
        advisors, 119–121
    income/job status of, 23, 24
    influence of opinions and
        recommendations, 124
    inventory of client base, 126
    purchases of, 117
    standard of living of, 24
    top turnoffs toward salespeople,
        125–126
    trustworthiness of advertising,
        118–121
    in the workforce, 24

Mental habits, 199
Mental rehearsal, 181–182, 191
Mercedes, 134
Millennial generation, 133, 135,
    138, 142, 148
Mind-set, affluent, 88
    distrustful, overcoming, 122–124
    I-can't-do-it, 202
    as impediment to salespeople,
        1669-170
    making changes using
        affirmations, 189
    pre- and post- crisis decision
        making, 21–23
    pre- and post- crisis lifestyle,
        23–24
    research facts, 24–25
    of salespeople, 17–19, 174
    taking action, 25
    trust factor in advertising, 17–21
Mini-close, 64, 65
Mistrust, in advertising, 80, 150
Mobile ads, 21
Model, sphere of influence, 44–45
Molloy, John T., 98, 108

N

Names, remembering, 103
Negative personal presence, 101
Network expansion, 49
Networking opportunities, 62–63
Net worth, of affluent household, 174
New York Times, 129, 152, 153
Nissan, 171
Nonaffluents. *See also* Consumers,
    nonaffluent
    spending of, 13
    standard of living of, 24
Nordstrom, 84, 85

O

Older affluents, 137, 139
Older generation, communication
    of, 140

O'Neal, Shaquille, 20
Online brand, protecting, 142
Online medical treatment, 154
Online presence, 143
Online profiling, 79
Online research, 148, 151–158
Online reviews, 152–153
Open posture, 102, 103
Opinions/recommendations, 155, 158
Opportunities:
  looking for, 93
  networking, 62–63
  past, revisiting, 66–67
  upmarket, creating, 171–172
Organization, emotional
    attachment to, 63

P
Parking, in environment checklist,
    112
Passion, trust in, 220
Patel, Gaurav, 29–30, 33, 43,
    44, 226
Patience, sales professionals
    and, 126
People, right, associating with,
    186–187
Performance rankings, 93
Personal, being, 34
Personal action, taking, 130
Personal appearance, assessing, 113
Personal branding, 107
Personal conversation, expanding
    from business to, 92
Personal development, personal
    commitment and, 221
Personal energy, 98
Personal gift, 32, 33
Personal information:
  to formulate questions, 92
  gathering, 40, 93
  uncovering, 83, 91, 130
Personal inspection/consultation,
    113, 155, 158

Personal intelligence gathering, 33,
    34, 37–38
Personalization, 83–85
Personalized business
    relationship, 39
Personalized communication, 140
Personalized products gifts, 36
Personalized services:
  demand of, 24
  differentiation through, 29–30
  good service and, 40
  ranking of, 13
  repeat purchases and, 70
Personal passion points gifts, 36
Personal presence:
  as mind-set, 170
  negative, 101
  power of, 100–101
  of top performers, modeling,
    106–107
Personal relationships:
  becoming social, 85–87
  building and cultivating, 75,
    87–88
  developing, 25, 122–123, 165
  digital impact, 88–90
  getting personal, 83–85
  keeping it simple and personal,
    91–92
  professional alliances, 81–83
  with prospective clients, 175
  referrals vs. introductions,
    76, 77–81
  research facts and taking
    action, 93
Personal service, 40, 150–151
Pfizer, advertising expenditure
    of, 20
Physical appearance, 98, 107, 112
Plan development, of best and
    potential clients, 14
Planning form, intimate event,
    55–56
Politicians, mirroring, 108

Positive impression, making, 136
Post-crisis decision making, 21–23
Posture, strong, maintaining, 103
Potential prospects, 49
Power pose/power posing,
    101–103, 107, 113, 181
Praise, 103
Pre- and post-crisis lifestyles, 23–24
Preparation phase, sales reluctance
    and, 180–181
Presence. *See also* Personal presence
    online, 143
    salespeople and, 99
Prices, consumers and, 228
Problems, solving, 224–226, 233
Products:
    asking personal questions linked
        to, 92
    delivery of, 22
    performed as expected, 40
    reassessing, 14
    trust in delivery of, 150
    understanding, 25
Professional alliances, 81–83
Professional relationships, 78
Profile/profiling:
    affluent clients, 5–6, 40, 71
    online, 79
    top referral alliance partners, 82
Proposals, creating, 165
Prospect(s):
    assessing qualified, 198
    social, 64–66
    tracking, 207, 211
Psychological fears, 172
*The Psychology of Sales Call
    Reluctance: Earning What
    You're Worth* (Dudley and
    Goodson), 178
Purchase decisions:
    Amazon Effect as factor in,
        147–150
    direct, 3–4, 7
    factors driving, 22, 150

Great Recession and, 117
    online reviews and, 152–153
    word-of-mouth influence and,
        49, 124
Purchase(s):
    power, household income and, 6
    repeat, 70, 141
Pushy follow-up, 69, 125

Q
Questions:
    answering naive, 126
    asking before completing
        transaction, 118
    to gather intelligence, 34
    personal, conversations and
        asking, 91–92

R
Rapport:
    building, 54
    development, salespeople and, 69,
        118, 126
Realtors, cultivating relationships
    with, 5
Reassessing products and
    services, 14
Reciprocity, law of, 32–33, 43
Recollection, 66
Recreational introduction
    approach, 79
"Redirect" marketing tactic,
    64, 65
Reed, Andrew E., 137
Referrals, 49, 76
    alliances, 81–82
    getting personal and, 93
    introductions *vs.*, 77–81
    sales and, 198
Rejection, fear of, 173
*Relationship Management/
    Relationship Marketing
    Nexus*™, 33, 48, 50, 53,
        78, 85

Relationship manager, 123–124
Relationship marketing, 75–76
Relationships, 5, 9. *See also*
    Personal relationships
    with affluent women, 126–127
    built on trust, developing, 22
    business, 76, 78
    business-and-personal, 7–8
    business-social, 86–87
    challenges of managing, 82–83
    intimate event and, 48–49
    professional, 78
    sales before, 68
    with salespeople, 76
    shift, 7
    vacations and enhancing, 35
Reminder call, purpose of, 53
Repeat business, good service and,
    39
Reputation
    of the company, 150, 159
    importance of, 231–232
Research, online, 148, 150–158
Responsiveness, 140, 142
Retail clients, sales to, 118
Reviews, online, 152–153
Ritz-Carlton-quality service, 233
Rosenthal, Elisabeth, 18

S
Sales, affluent, 98, 163, 232.
    See also Affluents sales
    opportunity; Sales reluctance,
    affluent
    activating achievement cycle,
        201–202
    before relationships, 68
    research facts, 217
    revisiting achievements of the
        past, 202–206
    selecting activities related to
        goals, 198–199
    staying on your critical path,
        206–212

taking action, 217–218
top performers, 104,
    105–107, 113
top professionals, traits of,
    212–216
Sales managers, 168, 169, 170
Salesperson/salespeople, 99, 106
    affluent consumers and,
        5, 17
    appearance of, 112
    conversation with, 70
    firm's advertising message and,
        125
    mind-set of, 17–19, 174
    overcoming distrustful mindset,
        122–124
    redirecting social contact,
        65–66
    relationship with, 76, 83–84
    social self-consciousness
        and, 191
    trust in, 4, 75
    ways to appear salesy, 67–69
    women and, 75, 128–129
Sales reluctance, affluents:
    causes of, 177–178
    controlling doubt, 183–190
    overcoming, 178–179
    as problem, 179–180
    research facts, 191
    taking action, 180–183
Salesy, ways salespeople appear,
    67–69, 71
Scripted, being too, 68
Selecting clients, 50
Self-Affirmation recording
    technique, 187–190
Self-awareness, 214–215
Self-made, affluent consumers
    as, 217
The Self-Talk Solution
    (Helmstetter), 201, 202
Seniors, 133
Servant, being, 226–227

Service(s). *See also* Personalized
  services
  asking personal questions linked
    to, 92
  beyond expectations, 39
  delivery of, 22, 42
  personal, 40, 150–151
  reassessing, 14
  trust in delivery of, 150
  understanding, 25
  "wow," 30–31
Shane Homes, 128
Shellenbarger, Sue, 102
Situational introduction
    approach, 79
Skype, 90
Smartphone owners, 70
Smartphones, 143
Social (business-casual) dress, of
    top performers, 105
Social events, 85–87, 93
Social groups, 62
Social introduction approach, 79
Social media:
  demographics adopting, 70
  generating buzz through, 43, 71
  getting comfortable with, 94
  as means of communication, 90
  selling commandment and
    embracing, 232–233
  use of, 58–61
  word-of-mouth influence
    through, 135–136
Social paths, to engage partners, 83
Social prospecting, 64–66, 69
Social relationship, 76, 78
Social self-consciousness, 178, 191
Spending:
  of the affluents, 6, 13, 217
  of households, 174, 217
  of the nonaffluents, 13
Spenner, Patrick, 149
Spheres of influence, 200
  of affluent family, 70, 71

model, 44–45
Spontaneous situational
    introduction approach, 79
Sporting events:, 51
Standard of living, 24, 217
Starbucks, 97, 232
Starting out right technique, 185
"The Star Treatment: Flying Like
    Jennifer Aniston"
    (McCartney), 87
Stevenson, Robert Louis, 197
Strategic networking, 63
Strategic placement introduction
    approach, 79
Streitfeld, David, 152, 153
"'Struggling' on $350,00 a Year"
    (Frank), 166
Success, 22
  in acquiring affluent clientele,
    163
  linking activities to goals and, 206
  through personalized service,
    29–30
Surprise and delight:
  affluent clients, 200
  as agenda item, 37
  ideas with great effect, 35–39
  initiative, 31–32, 33, 40
  quick tips, 34–35
Sutton, Willy, 163

T
Tablets, 143
Tag along introduction
    approach, 79
Talking too much, 67–68, 125
Tattoos, 106
Technology, staying current with,
    141, 142
Telephone communication, 93
"Tests Reveal Mislabeling of Fish"
    (Rosenthal), 18
The Wealth Report - Blog
    (Frank), 166

Think inexpensive, 34
Time Warner, 21, 222, 223
Timing, irregular, employing, 34
"To Keep Your Customers, Keep
    It Simple" (Spenner and
    Freeman), 149
Top performers, personal tips of,
    105–107
Top-quintile household, 6
Toughness, 169–170
Toyota, 171
Traits, of affluent sales
    professionals, 212–216
Trust, 3
    in advertising, 7, 19, 80–81,
        118–119, 150
    affluents and, 93
    in automotive advertising, 20
    building and gaining, 9,
        126, 149
    events and establishing, 48–50
    of product or service delivered,
        150
    in salespeople, 4, 75
Twitter, 232, 233
Two-step introduction approach, 79
2013 APD Research, 12, 124, 220,
    223, 226, 230, 232

U
Upmarket, moving:
    fear factor and, 163–166
    households with $250,000
        annual income, 166–167
    research facts, 174
    taking action, 174
    working affluent, 171–172
    worst fear exercise, 172–173

V
Vacations, 35
Value, defining and obtaining, 22
Value exceeding price,
    providing, 228

Verizon, advertising expenditure
    of, 21
Video, memorializing events with
    taking, 54, 59–60
Visibility campaign, 43, 61–62,
    70, 71
Visualizing daily affluent sales
    routine, 182
Visualizing goals, 204
Volvo, 134

W
Wall Street Journal, 87, 102, 166
Warranty/guarantee, 150, 230
Weekly activities, 204–205, 207,
    209–211, 212
Weekly metrics scorecard, 211
Welcome address, 54
Wenzel, Shane, 128
"What Do Women Want? Just Ask"
    (Meece), 128, 129
White paper by Cornell University,
    136–137
Women, affluent. See also Female of
    the household
    attire of, 104, 109–110
    attitude toward financial
        advisors, 119–121
    gift of gab, 124
    income/job status of, 23, 24
    influence of opinions and
        recommendations, 124
    modeling accessories of top
        performers, 105–106
    relationships with, 126–127
    research facts and taking
        action, 130
    salespeople and, 75, 128–129
    standard of living of, 24
    top turnoffs toward salespeople,
        125–126
    trustworthiness in,
        118–124
Woods, Tiger, 184

Word-of-mouth influence:
  gifts stimulating, 35
  lasting impression and, 107
  personal intelligence gathering
    and, 34
  purchase decision and, 22, 49,
    124, 148
  relying, 133
  reputation and, 231–232
  through social media, 135–136
  women and, 124
Workforce, affluent men and
  women in, 24
Working affluents:
  knowledge, 170–171
  mind-set, 169–170
  number of hours of, 168
  opportunities and, 171–172
Worry, avoiding, 198
Wow and Buzz, 54
  event, 46, 49
  leverage of social media, 59
  script used by, 53
  systematic approach of, 61
Wow factor gifts, 36–37

Wowing affluent clients:
  law of reciprocity, 32–33
  Patel's gas station, 29–30
  research facts, 39–40, 70
  surprise and delight, 31–32
  taking action, 40
  uncovering client information,
    34–39
  "wow" service experience, 30–31
"Wow" service experience, 30–31

X
X factor, 99

Y
Yahoo, 153
Yelp, 153
Younger affluents, 139
Young generation, 141
Young generation, communication
  of, 139–140
YouTube, 232, 233

Z
"Zombie salesmanship," 9